OLD VILLAGE LIFE

East Hagbourne Village

OLD VILLAGE LIFE

OR, GLIMPSES OF VILLAGE LIFE THROUGH ALL AGES

BY

P. H. DITCHFIELD, M.A., F.S.A.

F.R.S.L., F.R.Hist.S.

ORIEL COLLEGE, OXFORD; RECTOR OF BARKHAM, BERKSHIRE

WITH FORTY ILLUSTRATIONS AND PLANS

EP PUBLISHING LIMITED

1974

Republished © 1974 EP Publishing Limited
East Ardsley, Wakefield
Yorkshire, England
by kind permission of the copyright holders

This is a reprint of the second edition,
first published by Methuen & Co., London, 1921

ISBN 0 85409 994 8

Please address all enquiries to EP Publishing Limited
(address as above)

Printed in Great Brtiain by
REDWOOD BURN LIMITED
Trowbridge & Esher

PREFACE
TO THE FIRST EDITION

I HAVE tried in this volume to tell the story of village life in all the ages. It is an attractive study, especially for those whose duty or inclination has compelled them to live amongst the fields and lanes of rural England. Recently the country and the village have loomed large in the eyes of statesmen and the dwellers in towns. They used to neglect us, and think little of agriculture and of the struggles of the poor farmers and poorly paid peasants. So long as they received their corn cheaply from foreign lands, and were happy when the price was as low as 22s. a quarter, they cared not whether the landlord was ruined, the farmer starved, and the labourer emigrated to the towns or the colonies. Politically we were rather in disgrace. The squires were relics of feudalism, and ought to be suppressed and extinguished by heavy taxation; the farmers held unsound views, and were not sufficiently enamoured of reform and revolutionary schemes; and the labourers were too ignorant to understand political questions and to accept as Gospel truth all the statements of the reforming strangers.

But all that dark age has passed. The limelight has shone upon us, and we are rather startled by the unaccustomed glare. People have discovered that we have our uses, that when foreign ships bringing precious freights of corn were being torpedoed wholesale, and there was a danger of England being starved to death, and forced by famine to yield to an implacable foe who could not conquer us in any other way, the only salvation rested on the British farmers and their stout-hearted labourers. And they have not betrayed the trust reposed in them. They ploughed up their pastures and set to work with all their might to produce food for the nation, in spite of losing their best men, who went to fight and who proved themselves to be the bravest and staunchest soldiers. England owes a debt to us country folk which it will not be easy to repay.

We are still a little anxious. We want to know how long we can depend upon receiving good prices for our produce. But we are grateful for the attention which has been bestowed upon us. We hear on all sides theories for the reconstruction of village life, often advocated by people who are ignorant of rural conditions and economy. But no one is more eager than we are, who live in the country, for a true policy of reconstruction. We want to see our villages populous again, and not to lose all our best and brightest youths and see them flocking to the towns, while only the old labourers are left behind to till our fields. We want better cottages; not that we should see all the beautiful old rural dwellings, with their fine gables and thatched roofs and lovely gardens, pulled down and replaced by hideous modern cottages. It is quite possible to adapt these old buildings to modern needs. We want to have clubs and reading-rooms, more games and attractions in the village. The health of the nation requires that there should be a strong breed of country folk. When I was lecturing on country life in the heart of the East End of London, at Toynbee Hall, I talked with some of the men, and they told me that were it not for the influx of country people into London the race would die out. Let us try to bring back these people from the grim and dark streets of the city to rural life, to the fresh air and invigorating atmosphere of rustic scenes and surroundings, rather than merge our agricultural labourers, their wives and children, with the social communities of towns, their fœtid vapours and unhealthy dwelling-places.

One of the charms of the country is its unchanging character. It retains its relics of the past, which are obliterated in towns, and the best policy of reconstruction is to blend the new with the old. I prefer to reconstruct backwards, to see the Roman in his villa, which usually stood on the site of the present manor-house; the Saxon thane and the Norman lord; the monks at their country grange gathering in their corn in their huge barns; the mediæval labourers in the fields; the revival of agriculture in Tudor and Stuart times; the old methods of farming; the customs, games, and pastimes of the villagers—all these interest me; and when I walk through the fields and lanes they are as real to me as the squire, farmer, and peasant who now dwell around me. I will endeavour to introduce them to you, and to look back a little before we look forward and welcome the changes which wise men are devising for our improvement and betterment.

Our survey of early times, of prehistoric folk, of Roman and Saxon times, will be but brief. I have already endeavoured to treat of these in another book. We shall try to dwell more particularly on the Tudor and Stuart times, and also on the developments of the eighteenth and nineteenth centuries. In building up the new order we must lay it on the old foundations. These we shall try to trace, and though the modern reformers seem to fix their eyes on the construction of garden cities that are deemed to be earthly Paradises, it is worth while to discover how the old village communities lived and prospered in ancient days, and to learn how to graft new branches upon the aged trunks. Such trees may produce better fruit than quite new seedlings.

It is perhaps fitting that I should write this book, as from this rectory more than a hundred years ago went out a remarkable work written by a remarkable man, the Rev. Dr. David Davies. He is reputed to be, with Sir Frederick Eden, the chief authority on social questions relating to agricultural affairs in the eighteenth century. This book is called *The Case of the Labourers in Husbandry,* and it made a great impression upon the men of his time, and if his conclusions had been acted upon and his advice taken many of the subsequent evils might have been avoided. It would have rejoiced his heart if he could have foreseen the present rise in wages and the better conditions of the agricultural labourer.

I have written already several books on village life, chiefly from an antiquary's or from an architectural point of view. In this volume, although archæological subjects could not be entirely excluded, I have dwelt mainly on the conditions of the villagers in the different periods culminating in the troubles of the eighteenth and nineteenth centuries and in the hopes and ideals of the new age which is now dawning upon rural life. I have consulted many authorities, whose works I hope that I have duly acknowledged in the text and footnotes.

P. H. DITCHFIELD

BARKHAM RECTORY
BERKSHIRE
1920

PREFACE
TO THE SECOND EDITION

THE demand for a new edition of this book has enabled me to make a few slight alterations and additions which I hope will increase the accuracy and usefulness of the work. I am glad to discover that the lovers of old village life have found it helpful and interesting, and am grateful to many correspondents who have kindly written to me and to the reviewers for their generous reception of the volume.

P. H. D.

CONTENTS

LIST OF ILLUSTRATIONS

ILLUSTRATIONS IN THE TEXT

OLD VILLAGE LIFE

OLD VILLAGE LIFE

CHAPTER I

PREHISTORIC PEOPLES

Introduction—Prehistoric times—Eolithic—Palæolithic—Neolithic—Dolichocephalic—Brachycephalic—Celts—Goidels—Brythons.

EXCEPT in the large, overgrown, populous villages of the North, or in the Black Country of the Midlands, the kindly earth of our rural hamlets has carefully and reverently preserved relics and traces of their former inhabitants. They do not forget old friends, even after the lapse of some thousands of years, and the presence of prehistoric camp or earthwork, tumulus or implement of warfare or of toil, testifies to the existence of remote ancestors who trod the same fields wherein we labour to-day, and who hunted in our woods strange creatures that have long ago disappeared. It is an antiquary's delight to explore the buried past, and to try to recall the scenes that were enacted long ago on spots familiar to him. Nothing delights a village audience more than to tell them something of the story of their home, and of the people who lived in bygone times in the old manor-house, and whose monuments in the church record their memories.

I know a lane in which some of the Royalist troopers fell upon a company of Cromwell's soldiers, and there was some hard fighting, and several men were killed or wounded; and my horse pricks up his ears as if he smelt the battle from afar and saw the ghosts of warriors long deceased contending in the narrow, tree-hung lane. A page in a village register records the burial of "souldiers" slain in some skirmish of which history takes no cognisance. It is pleasant to recall the scenes of bygone village life and compare them with the present. Village life is sometimes very dull and monotonous; but the war aroused us from our slumbers. We have been very busy and active during the last five years, and reformers are coming to us and telling us how we may revive our village life and make it so attractive that our young men will not flock to the towns out of sheer boredom; and they will "see visions and our old men dream dreams" of a happy and prosperous countryside, and of everything being perfectly right in this best of possible worlds. So mote it be.

Few people realise the immense antiquity of civilisation in this country. Our history books usually begin with Julius Cæsar's attempt to conquer Britain in the year 55 B.C.; but our prehistoric monuments extend our gaze to a very far-distant horizon. The earth has preserved traces of such early denizens as those who are styled Eolithic, Palæolithic, and Glacial men, though little is known about them, save that their flint implements are often discovered, and reveal something of their character and modes of life. Palæolithic man was a nomad, and lived by hunting powerful and wild animals: the mammoth, brown and grizzly bears, rhinoceros, hippopotamus, urus, bison, red deer, and other creatures which wandered into our island across a narrow stream that divided us from the Continent. But these men have left little trace of any rudimentary ideas of civilisation. It is, however, different with their successors, the Neolithic man, who was much more civilised, and was of a much higher type. Evidences of this we shall discover later. He grew corn to make bread, and brought with him to this island cows and sheep and goats, horses and dogs. He made pottery, moulding the clay with his hand and baking it in a fire. He could spin thread and weave stuffs, and was not inferior—some authorities deem him to have been far superior—to the Saxon and Dane who carried fire and sword into our peaceful hamlets and towns many centuries later.

No one can assert exactly when Neolithic man first settled in this country. He was certainly here about 1,800 years B.C.—*i.e.*, about 3,000 or 4,000 years ago—carrying on his simple pastoral life, worshipping the Sun god, building the great sun temple of Stonehenge and other megalithic monuments. This is, indeed, looking backwards. Men were working here on our hills and in the vales, keeping their flocks of sheep, milking their cows, and driving their wooden ploughs, before the Israelites left Egypt, four centuries before the Siege of Troy, eight centuries before Rome was founded, and a thousand years before the Battle of Marathon. It seems almost inconceivable.

These Neolithic folk were long-headed men and women, styled dolichocephalic, the back of their skulls being strangely prolonged. They were dark-complexioned, of small stature, about five feet six inches in height, and their descendants are the Iberian or Basque races in the Western Pyrenees, in the West of Ireland, and in parts of Wales. They were conquered by another wave of invaders, the Bronze men—that is, the people who had discovered the use of bronze, an alloy of copper and tin, for the making of weapons and implements. Their skulls were round, and they are named brachycephalic; they are believed to have belonged to the original Aryan race, whose birthplace was Southern Asia. They are usually termed Celts, and peering into the mists of these far-off ages we think we have discovered two Celtic invasions, the Goidels and the Brythons. The latter were the ancestors of the modern Welsh and Cornishmen, answering to the description I have just given of the Bronze men, while the former were bigger and stronger and have as their descendants the sandy-haired Gaelic-speaking Scot. A later Celtic invasion was made by the Belgæ, who were here when the Romans came, and we open the first page of our history books, though we fail to learn very much from its perusal, and have to rely to a great extent for our knowledge on the spade of the antiquary and careful archæological research.

CHAPTER II

PREHISTORIC EARTHWORKS

Earthworks — Tribal boundaries — Fortresses — Destruction of earthworks—Icknield Way—Uffington Castle—Camps—Pit-dwellings—Barrows—Weyland Smith's Cave—Cæsar's Camps—Classification of forts—Successive occupation—Promontory forts—Strength of the entrances—Cambridge-shire dykes—Offa's Dyke—Grim's Dykes—Dane's ditches.

AFTER this brief survey of the various races who have seen fit to invade our island, it may be well to examine some of the traces of their presence and the works they have left behind. These are so numerous that it is not improbable that in the neighbourhood of your own village you will be able to discover some earthwork or other relic of the primitive inhabitants of Britain. This, perhaps, you may be able to explore, having sought some expert guidance, so as not to destroy important features nor to miss any object that ought to have been recorded. A few years ago I was lecturing on rural antiquities to a village audience, and I exhibited some views of flint implements and other treasures. This fired the imagination of some of the ladies present, who set to work and discovered many similar objects, then found some Roman tiles and tesseræ; and this led to the finding of a Roman villa of a very interesting type, which was duly excavated under expert guidance, and a museum was built by the generous gift of Viscount Hambleden for all the treasures and Roman relics that were unearthed. Thus a very useful crop grew up from a very small seed. It is quite possible that in your neighbourhood similar happy results may be obtained.

Earthworks are extraordinarily numerous in England, and a very large number remain to be explored. They are of various kinds, and testify to the quarrelsomeness of our primitive forefathers, and to the necessity for them to defend themselves against robbers or opposing tribes or troublesome beasts. The face of the country is scarred with tribal boundaries, dykes, ditches, embankments, as well as fortified camps and enclosures, and other kinds of defences. The makers of these skilfully adapted natural advantages of situation for the purpose of strengthening their positions. Thus we find fortresses partly inaccessible by reason of precipices, cliffs, or water, defended only in part by artificial works. and other fortresses on hilltops following the natural lines of the hills with carefully constructed artificial defences. Then there are rectangular enclosures, and others of simple plan, including all forts and towns of the Romano-British period.

Forts consisting only of a mount with encircling moat or fosse, and fortified mounts, wholly or partly artificial, with the remains of an attached court or bailey, or sometimes with two or more such courts, belong mainly to the Norman period. Manor-houses and farmsteads often surrounded themselves with moats, forming artificial islands, thus affording some protection from outlaws or wild beasts; and when this simple mode of defence was not considered strong enough, additional fortifications were added, and stronger defensive works constructed, ramparted and fossed, and in some instances the enclosures were provided with outworks. Nor were these defences confined to individual houses. Ancient village sites were sometimes protected by walls, ramparts, or fosses. This classification of earthworks has been drawn up by the Earthworks Committee of the Congress of Archæological Societies of which I have been a member since its inauguration more than a decade ago, and many active and careful observers have been engaged in exploring, drawing plans, and recording examples of these various kinds of earthen defences found in all parts of the country, and trying to save them from destruction.

The farmer's plough often is a deadly enemy to these ancient earthworks, especially in these days when we are asked and ordered to turn our grass fields into arable land, and the ploughshare has no mercy on these relics of old-world folk who have long ago passed away. As the old antiquary grumbled in the *Scouring of the White Horse:* "They are all mad for ploughing, sir, these blockhead farmers. They would plough and grow mangold-wurzels on their fathers' graves. The Tenth Legion, sir, has probably marched along this road: Severus and Agricola have ridden along it, sir: Augustine's monks have carried the Cross along it. There is that in that old mound and ditch which the best turnips and oats in the world can't replace."

During a hard winter several years ago a kind farmer, in order to provide work for his men, employed them in digging up a very famous earthen rampart near Wallingford, in Berkshire, that was of considerable importance. He was a little too kind and generous, and one wishes that his generosity had been turned into another direction. Constantly the number of these works is being diminished, and those that remain should be most carefully guarded and, whenever possible, preserved.

I happen to have a more intimate acquaintance with Berkshire earthworks than with those of other counties, and will venture to draw my illustrations from that shire. We have a great store of these. Across Northern Berkshire, overlooking the beautiful Vale of the White Horse, fairest and loveliest of valleys and not unrenowned in story, runs the old British trackway, the Icknield Way, or the Way of the Iceni, stretching from East Anglia to Gloucestershire. Guarding its course and in its neighbourhood are scores of so-called camps or fortified enclosures. These primitive fortresses usually follow the shape of the hills on which they stand.

Such is Uffington Castle on the Berkshire Downs, not a great old stone building with a moat and round towers and battlements, but a large space surrounded by a bank of earth or vallum, eight or ten feet high in some places, but lower at others;

and outside this a great, broad ditch or fosse which is again defended by another bank. There is but one gateway on the west, where the bank is curved round so as to form a sort of guard-room. Some round holes were discovered in the rampart years ago, wherein doubtless small tree trunks were

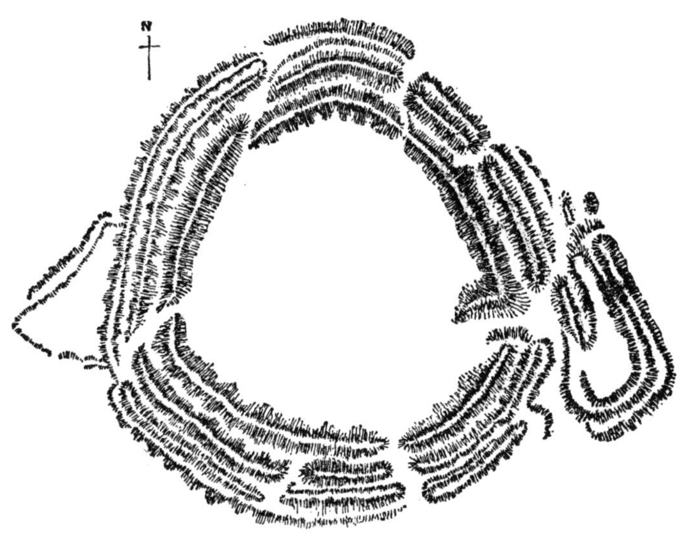

PLAN OF YARNBURY CASTLE, WILTS
(From Windle's *Prehistoric Age*)

inserted as a basis for wattle-work palisading as an additional defence. The makers of these camps were very clever and ingenious in guarding the entrances, and in devising snares and pitfalls to deceive an enemy. Perhaps the latter would discover a gateway into the fortress that seemed not to be well guarded. A band of doughty warriors would rush in, only to find a blind alley, while from the banks above heavy stones and arrows with sharp flint heads and murderous javelins would be showered down upon them. The plan of Yarnbury Castle, Wilts, shows clearly the intricate and ingenious nature of these defences.

What was the object of these camps? In an earlier book I stated that they were places of refuge whither the tribe could retire when threatened by the advent of an enemy. The makers of them were pastoral people, and their flocks grazed on the downs and hillsides. When their scouts brought news of the advance of a hostile force, some signal would be given by the blowing of a horn, and the people would at once flee to their fortress driving their cattle before them, and awaiting there the advent of their foes. The Blowing Stone that now stands in front of an inn at Sparsholt, having been removed from some place near Uffington Castle, is generally supposed to have been an instrument that was used for this purpose. It is a square block of sarsen stone with a natural hole or funnel, and if you are skilled in the art you can blow through this hole, and a deep, low, booming sound wails forth, and can be heard for a long distance.

Although this camp on the Berkshire Downs was probably used for the purpose I have stated, since my book was written antiquaries seem to have generally adopted the theory that these camps were not merely places of refuge, but permanent dwelling-places. In many of the enclosures there are the remains of pit-dwellings or habitations formed by digging holes in the ground and roofing them over with a light thatch. I have described these at some length in my former book on *English Villages*,[1] and need not repeat what I have therein stated. But these primitive dwellings show that these camps were not merely camps of refuge, but the towns or villages of Neolithic folk who lived there about 3,000 years ago; and also later relics prove that their successors, the Celts, made their homes in the same pit-huts guarded by the same ramparts.

Near these camps there is often a Neolithic tumulus or barrow, the place of burial of some tribal chieftain. There is one at Uffington known as Weyland Smith's Cave, to which a strange and curious story is attached. The grave is known as a long barrow or chambered cairn, and was certainly made by Neolithic men; but Weyland the Smith was a metal-worker, and belongs to Scandinavian legend and sagas. These tell us of the myth of the Sun-horse, a white steed called Gravie, ridden by Sigurd, and shod by Weiland the Smith god. Hence it must be, as my friend Colonel Haines has pointed out, that at some time, long after the building of the barrow, some Scandinavian folk came to the Berkshire Downs and associated the old grave with the legend of Weiland, and called it the redoubtable Smith's forge. He thinks also that the horse must also have been dug out by them, but this is conjectural.

There are many so-called Cæsar's camps in England, though Julius Cæsar never saw them,

[1] *English Villages*, p. 33.

and these were made long before his attempt to conquer Britain, though the Romans used them. We have one in Berkshire, the only important earthwork in the eastern portion of our county. It lies upon the edge of a high plateau, and its ramparts follow the contours of the ground, producing a camp somewhat like an oak leaf. There

BRITISH CAMP, HEREFORDSHIRE BEACON, MALVERN
(From Windle's *Prehistoric Age*)

is another and more famous Cæsar's camp at Aldershot, owing to its modern military renown, which was in existence at least a thousand years before the Roman conqueror's time; and there is another at Folkestone, deemed by old antiquaries to have been a Roman pharos, which is certainly of the Norman period. Indeed, one has to unlearn much that was formerly taught us with assertions of authority. An illustration is given of the famous Herefordshire Beacon, near Malvern, which was a British camp. It obtained its present name of Beacon because it was used in later times as a place for a bonfire to arouse the county in case of invasion, as when the Armada threatened England. You will remember Macaulay's spirited poem on the chain of bonfires that summoned all Englishmen to defend their country as each fire was lighted—

From Eddystone to Berwick bounds, from Lynn to Milford Bay.

In this camp the central defended portion is small, but the outward earthworks include a large part of the hill. Its exact date has not been determined, but the discovery of objects of the Bronze Age near it seems to show that the earthworks belong to the Celtic period. In old maps and guide-books camps are positively assigned to different races on very slender evidence. If a camp is circular it is called British; if rectangular, it is pronounced Roman; if oval, Danish. But these distinctions are entirely fallacious. One old antiquary allowed his imagination to run riot. He attributed one of the Cornish "Rounds" to the Saxons, who constructed it for their ladies to exercise themselves in walking unobserved by common folk!

Professor Windle has summed up the matter very wisely thus: "There was the strongly fortified hill-camp, intended as a place of resort in emergency, but not as a place of habitation. It was a place to which the inhabitants of the valley betook themselves with their families and their herds when attacked by enemies, but a place reserved for such occasions, and, perhaps on account of its bleakness, or its want of water, unsuitable and unintended for a protracted occupation. Then there was the village surrounded by low banks and ditches, of little use for purposes of defence, but subserving other ends, perhaps as cattle-folds, or means of drainage. And, finally, there was the third class, where, because the local climate, the water-supply, and the general topographical conditions were all favourable, the town was also a camp, and served the purposes of a habitation and a fortress."

I have said that some of these fortresses were inhabited by successive races. Old Sarum is a good example of this. It was probably pre-Roman originally. The Romans used it as a fortress; it was a Saxon burh, a Norman stronghold containing a cathedral and a castle, and a mediæval city, retaining until modern times its right to send a member to Parliament, though there were only three electors. Some of these old primitive earthworks have been used by belligerents in mediæval warfare and in Cromwell's time; and perhaps, but for the mercy of God and the strength of the British Navy, if the Germans had succeeded in landing upon our shores, they would have been useful again in repelling the invaders.

Some of them have been styled Promontory Forts, which category includes the so-called "cliff castles," such as the Trevalgue Head on the coast of Cornwall, Trevarrian, Bedruthan, and Park Head. Nearly all these cliffs on the Cornish coast have prehistoric fortifications. Sometimes coast castles were probably constructed by invaders, who thus secured their *point d'appui* on the country on which they had landed. Such is Flamborough Head, which is entrenched by Dane's Dyke. Promontory camps were also formed inland on hills, protected on one side by precipices or steep escarpments, and on the others by banks and ditches. An example of this is seen in the camp on Bredon Hill, Gloucestershire.

I have written of the attention which their founders paid to increase the strength of the entrances to these strongholds. One of the most ingenious and complicated is that of Maiden Castle, Dorset. The attackers must have required almost as much ingenuity as the solvers of the Maze at Hampton Court. Another important class of earthworks are the long lines of fortifications which extend for miles across the country, and must have entailed vast labour in their construction. These ramparts were doubtless tribal boundaries, or fortifications used by one tribe against another. The Cambridgeshire dykes are tremendous earthworks, which bar the route from the Thames Valley into Norfolk. They consist of a deep ditch dug down some fifteen feet into chalk, the material thrown up so as to form a bank or vallum. There is the Balsham or Fleam Dyke, Pampisford Dyke, and others, such as the Brent or Brant, Heydon, Wood Street, Devil's Dyke, Black Ditch, Devil's Ditch, known also as the Foss Dyke. At my request the late learned Professor T. McKenny Hughes wrote a long description of these,[1] and he came to the conclusion that they were erected by British tribes who were constantly at war with each other. The Iceni fought the Girvii, the Trinobantes opposed the Cassivellauni, and then the Romans subdued them all, and possibly the fair-haired Scandinavians and the red-haired North Germans added further elements of strife. A terrible slaughter took place in the war ditches, where 80,000 natives were said by Tacitus[2] to have been killed, and the Professor found many skeletons of young and old lying in the ditch with limbs and head sometimes detached from the trunk, as if they had been left unburied.

These earthworks are common features of the defences of the British and pre-Roman tribes, but are not so common in association with Roman or Saxon times. You will perhaps remind me of Offa's Dyke on the Welsh borders, but there is strong reason for supposing that Offa only adapted for his use against the Welsh the system of defence that had been constructed by various tribes long before his time. All over England there are many other dykes. There are twenty-two Grim's Dykes. The name was probably derived from Grim, the Saxon devil, or evil spirit; and it was bestowed upon these mysterious monuments of an ancient race, which the Saxons found in various parts of their conquered country. Unable to account for the existence of these vast mounds and fortresses,

[1] *Journal of the British Archæological Association*, vol. xix., New Series, p. 135, etc.

[2] *Annals*, xii. 31.

lines of fortification, and roads, they attributed them to satanic agency. There is a Grime's Dyke, or Græme's Ditch, near Watford in Hertfordshire, a Devil's Dyke, near Brighton, a Devil's Highway leading from Staines to Silchester, a Grimmer's Dike, running through the Berkshire parishes of Ufton, Padworth, and Aldermarston, nearly to Silchester. A Grim's Dyke runs across the southern extremity of Oxfordshire from Henley to Mongewell, ten miles in length, and parallel with it, there is a Medlers-bank, exceeding it in length by nearly a third. I may mention the Roman rig that coasts the face of the hills all the way from Sheffield to Mexborough. It is advisable to beware of things and places styled Roman. Our forefathers called everything Roman which they did not understand. There is a "Roman camp" at Shelford, which is probably only a mediæval moated house; and we must be careful about Danes' ditches, or Danes' fields, and suchlike names, as the places may have no connection with the inhabitants of Denmark, but with Danet, an old name for the Devil or Grim.

CHAPTER III

BURIAL MOUNDS

Tumuli or barrows—Long barrow—Chambered tumuli—Weyland Smith's Cave—Round barrows—Contents of graves—Position of bodies.

ANOTHER very common form of earthwork are the tumuli, barrows, or burial mounds, which constitute an endless source of information with regard to the early inhabitants of our island. The subject is a very large one, and if I were to attempt to treat it fully I should be obliged to devote the rest of this book, with sundry other additional volumes for a full elucidation. The contents of the graves disclose much about the habits and modes of life of the various peoples, as they were accustomed to deposit in them curious objects, such as personal ornaments, weapons, pottery, and food, showing that they believed fully in a future existence, and were desirous of providing the dead with objects that might be useful to them in their life after death. This custom of placing strange things in graves existed until quite recently. In the days of my predecessor, about half a century ago, an old woman requested before she died that the following articles should be placed in her coffin: a snuff-box, umbrella, walking-stick, a threepenny-piece, a razor and shaving-box!

Burial customs prevail in many climes, and to cover the dead with a mound of earth was a custom common to all nations. All over Europe, in Northern Asia, India, and in the new world of America, we find burial mounds. The pyramids of Egypt are only glorified mounds, and our islands contain an endless variety, sometimes consisting of cairns, or heaps of stones, sometimes of huge hills of earth, one hundred and thirty feet in height and covering five acres, as at Silbury, Wilts; while others are only small heaps of soil a few feet high.

The contents of the barrows vary. Some people used to cremate the bodies of the deceased, and others buried them without cremation. Inhumation was the primitive practice; the burning of bodies came in later, but both methods of disposing of the dead were in use, and cremation never became a universal practice. During the Neolithic and Bronze Ages the people used both methods. Canon Greenwell, who is one of the chief authorities on barrows, having examined a vast number of these mounds, thus sums up his experiences:

> In Derbyshire the proportion is slightly in favour of burnt bodies; in Wiltshire burnt bodies are as three to one unburnt; in Dorsetshire as four to one; and in Cornwall cremation seems to have been by far the most common usage. In the counties of Denbigh, Merioneth, and Caernarvon cremation seems to have been almost universal. In Northumberland I have disinterred 71 bodies, and of these 55 were after cremation, and 26 by inhumation—the proportion of burnt to unburnt bodies being, therefore, almost two to one.

There are various kinds of barrows. The earliest is the Long Barrow, which class of tomb was formed by the Neolithic race, the long-headed, dolichocephalic people whose acquaintance we have already made. These barrows are of two forms—the chambered and the unchambered. The former consists of a central, cave-like chamber composed of large stones set upright on their edges with another large stone acting as a roof. This is called a cist. Leading into this cist is a passage composed of large stones with chambers in the form of transepts on either side. Many bodies could be placed in these receptacles, and the whole was covered with a mound of earth. In cases where the chamber is no wider than the passage or corridor, the sepulchre becomes a long rectangular gallery, and answers to the French *allée couverte*. Sometimes the chamber and passage were surrounded by a circle of stones, and the barrow by a trench and mound, the purpose of which is supposed to have been to keep the dead person from injuring the living. Weyland Smith's Cave is a good example of a Neolithic burial, the cist with its passage and transepts forming the figure of a cross. But there are several varieties of these chambered barrows. In some instances the transepts are reduplicated, and in others there is no central passage.

An illustration is given of the entrance to the Long Barrow at Uley, Gloucestershire, which has four chambers opening off the central avenue. This entrance is low, and the barrow is surrounded by a ring of stone. We also show the entrance to the remarkable Long Barrow at West Kennett, Wiltshire, the outer circle of which was removed by one Farmer Green, who plundered the Avebury avenues and circles to make boundary stones for his sheep-walks.

The construction of these chambered tumuli

ENTRANCE TO LONG BARROW, ULEY, GLOUCESTERSHIRE
(From Windle's *Prehistoric Age*)

necessitated the use of large stones. Where these were not available the builders usually erected a low wall, but no chambers, and the bodies were covered, after they had been burnt, by the mound. Round barrows were made by the Bronze men, and usually occur in groups. We have the Seven Barrows in Berkshire, near Faringdon, so named, though there are many more than seven. The body was placed in a grave and then a mound of earth was heaped upon it. Then a little later another burial took place on the top of the mound, and

ENTRANCE TO LONG BARROW, WEST KENNETT
(From Windle's *Prehistoric Age*)

another layer of earth added. The process was continued until the barrow assumed a considerable height. As I have said, many objects were buried with the bodies, and the bones of animals, perhaps the relics of funeral feasts, are found in these mounds. If I were confining this book to barrows I should have to record the contents of the graves, the kind of pottery in which the burnt ashes of the deceased were placed, the position of the bodies, which was usually crouching, the mournful burials of mother and infant, of husband and wife clasping each other's hands, and much else of the lore of prehistoric burial customs. Perhaps some day I may attempt to return to a subject that teems with interest, but may not be discussed further here.

CHAPTER IV

MEGALITHIC MONUMENTS

Megalithic monuments — Menhirs — Dolmens — Alignments — Cromlechs—Hoar stones—Avebury—Rollright Stones—Stonehenge.

RECENT investigations have shown the very wide extent of Megalithic monuments introduced by stone-using immigrants in all inhabited regions of the earth. Professor Elliot Smith and Dr. Rivers have discovered definite evidence of a widespread movement of people who built these great stone structures wherever they went.[1] These are found along the shores of the Mediterranean, in Western Asia, Egypt, Oceania, India, Indonesia, etc., as well as in our islands. These monuments are of various kinds: The menhir[2] is a tall rough pillar with the base fixed in the earth. The trilithon is a pair of tall stones set a short distance apart supporting a third stone laid across the top, such as you can see at Stonehenge. The dolmen is a sort of stone table, a large single stone slab being supported by several others, so as to form a chamber similar to the sepulchral cist which I have already described. The alignment is a series of menhirs arranged in open line so as to form a row or boundary

[1] *The Megalithic Culture of Indonesia*, by W. J. Perry, p. 2.

[2] The word is derived from the Celtic *men*, a stone, and *hir*, tall.

STONEHENGE

(From Windle's *Prehistoric Age in England*)

of a road or path. The cromlech consists of a number of menhirs arranged to enclose a space, either circular, ellipitical, or rectangular. These definitions explain the meaning of most of the principal types of Megalithic monuments that have been left to us by prehistoric folk. Great labour was exercised and much skill was necessary to produce these wonderful structures such as Stonehenge, which has been enrolled amongst the wonders of the world, and in the neighbourhood of many of our villages one or other of these relics of the former inhabitants may be seen.

Many questions suggest themselves. How did they contrive to erect such mighty monuments? How did they move such huge masses of stones? For what purpose did they erect them? Some of these queries it is difficult to answer. It may be safely conjectured that they nearly all relate to memorials of the dead and to the worship of the sun. The erection of single stones (menhirs) may have been connected with some important event or as a boundary stone. In England they are frequently called "hoar stones," the word *hoar* meaning a boundary; but their use as boundaries may have arisen long after their erection, and may in no way be connected with their original object. They usually were erected as memorials of the dead, and were set up together with other Megalithic forms, such as dolmens and alignments. In the Bible we read that Joshua commanded the Israelites to set up stones as a memorial of their passage through the Jordan, and Jacob and Laban raised a heap of stones upon Mount Gilead as a witness of their covenant. In Indonesia menhirs were set up to commemorate a league of peace between two tribes, or as offering-places.

In Gloucestershire there is the Hoar Stone near Lower Swell. Sometimes people have attached curious names to these menhirs. In the same shire, near Minchinhampton, there stands the "Woeful Dane's Bottom," the "Tingle Stone" near Avening, and the "Whittle Stone" near Lower Swell. In Devonshire we find the "Bair Down Man" near Princetown. The "Hoar Stone" near Steeple Aston, Wilts, with which his nurse used to frighten a young friend of mine by telling him that a devil lurked there, and a similar one at Enstone in Oxfordshire, are probably ruined dolmens.

Of cromlechs we have a large number in the British Isles. There is the well-known example at Avebury, which was superior to Stonehenge before it was mutilated by farmers who purloined the stones for gateposts and did other damage. It is also much earlier than its great rival on Salisbury Plain, as its stones are entirely unhewn. It is surrounded by a vallum and fosse, and has an area of twenty-eight acres. Within this earthen circle there is a circle of stones which encloses two smaller circles, each with a smaller concentric circle within it, and a stone erection, probably originally a dolmen, in the centre. There are two entrances to the cromlech which were approached by a passage guarded on each side by an alignment or row of stones.

Rollright Stones, in Oxfordshire, is another important cromlech, about which much folk-lore has gathered. It is found in the mediæval compilers of the *Marvels of Britain,* and is described as the second wonder of the realm. There is a circle of stone about one hundred feet in diameter, a menhir outside the circle, and still farther off a dolmen, styled the "Whispering Knights." The story is that a certain King was marching with his army when he met a witch to whom the ground belonged. He was on the crest of the hill from which the village of Long Compton would be visible in the combe below, when she stopped him with the words:

> Seven long strides shalt thou take and
> If Long Compton thou canst see
> King of England thou shalt be.

The King, who now thought his success assured, cried out exultingly:

> Stick, stock, stone,
> As King of England I shall be known!

So he took seven strides, but lo! but instead of looking down on Long Compton, there rose before him a long mound, and the witch said:

> As Long Compton thou canst not see
> King of England thou shalt not be.
> Rise up, stick, and stand still, stone,
> For King of England thou shalt be none,
> Thou and thy men hoarstones shall be
> And I myself an eldern-tree.

The doom was immediately consummated, but it is said that some day when England is in sore straits the spell will be broken, and the King will start as an armed warrior at the head of his army, conquer his enemies and rule over all the land. Sir Arthur Evans, whose version of the legend I have told, thinks that this may refer to Arthur at Avilion. The Witch-Elder still watches over the victims of her magic. Sir Arthur was told that the King and the Whispering Knights, who were traitors plotting against the King, used to go down the hill at midnight to drink of a spring, just as the stones of Carnac rush down to the sea on Christmas Eve. Moreover, the stones for a moment at midnight become men, join hands, and dance round in the air. Many other tales are associated with the stones. We owe the discovery of the origin of the name Rollright to Sir Arthur Evans's ingenious speculations. The name appears in Domesday as Rollandri, or the right of Roland, the great Christian hero who fought against the Saracens in the eighth century A.D., and Sir Arthur has shown that throughout Europe it was the custom to attach the name of the hero to ancient sites and objects. It is interesting to know that some English Saxon brought with him the legend from across the seas, and transferred it to our stone circle.

If space permitted, I should like to describe at length the great Stonehenge. I find a learned paper in *Archæologia* by Mr. Gowland on the subject who has said all that can be said. Some people express great wonder at the size of the monoliths, and imagine that they must have been conveyed to the spot from some vast distance; but these are the local sarsen stones that are found in abundance in the neighbourhood. Some igneous or "blue" stones were used in the construction of the cromlechs, but these were ice-borne boulders brought here by glaciers. According to the notions of the old curator the mighty stones stood here before the Deluge, and he used to point out (to his own satisfaction) signs of the action of water upon the stones, showing the direction in which the Flood "came rushing in." The date of the erection of this mighty Megalithic monument goes back to the very beginning of the Bronze Age, about 2000–1800 B.C. Sir Norman Lockyer worked out the problem mathematically and came to the conclusion that 1680 B.C., with a possible error of 200 years, was the correct date. It is well that antiquaries and astronomers should be of the same mind. Stonehenge has been private property for a long period. Recently it was purchased by Mr. Cobb and generously presented to the nation.

There is much else to record of village prehistoric antiquities. We have turf-cut monuments such as the White Horses cut out on the chalk downs, the curious cup-and-ring markings on rocks, the various kinds of pottery, the implements ranging from Palæolithic hammers to Celtic swords, brooches, shields, torques, horse-trappings, and much else.

I should like, as a modest collector, to have exhibited some flint implements, such as you may discover in your own fields or beds of gravel; but we have to examine the story of the village in all ages, and must at once abandon prehistoric times.

The Colchester Vase, showing Gladiators Fighting

CHAPTER V

THE VILLAGE IN ROMAN TIMES

The origin of villages—Popular ignorance of the Roman occupation of Britain—Continuity of village life—The villa—British agriculture—Types of Roman houses—Villa at Winchcombe—Basilical type—Life in a villa—*Villa Rustica* —Roads—Walls—Religion—Christianity.

HOW came our villages to be planted where they are? Did some good or evil angel scatter them about our countryside, as a farmer sows his seed in the fields? We may be sure that it was not chance which led our forefathers to plant their homesteads where they are. There must have been some reason for selecting the sites for their homes. And no one can tell exactly how old they are, and who founded them. We find their names in the Domesday Survey, and are proud of seeing our own village therein described with its owner, its number of freemen and socmen, and villains and borderers or cottagers and slaves; but that is quite modern compared with the actual age of the hamlet. Then we look into Abbey Chronicles and find Charters which tell of a still earlier time, the ninth or tenth century perhaps, when the village stood and was given to God and the Blessed Virgin and the Saints and the Abbot and monks serving God in some monastic house by some pious donor with threats of awful punishment for those who would dare to deprive the Abbey of this gift. But earlier still the story can be traced. As I have said, the Neolithic folk dwelt mainly in their guarded forts, in pit-dwellings on the hills, or pile-dwellings by some river bank. It would not be safe to ascribe to them any early attempts at town or village planning. But when the Bronze and Iron Ages came and the Celtic tribes flowed over Britain in all probability they were the original founders of our villages. They were agriculturists. They kept cows and sheep and horses, and farmed and tilled their lands; they left the fortified villages of their predecessors, and in the pleasant valleys built their homes.

The first necessity in choosing the site of their village was water. Hence they fixed their habitations on the banks of a stream, or where perpetual springs bubbled out from the hills, or where ponds or lakes seemed likely to supply their needs. Sinking wells belongs to a much later period. Hence we find that ancient villages always nestle beside some babbling brook or stream, though they generally avoid the banks of great rivers like the Thames, fearing the floods that would overwhelm them. A recent writer in my Journal,[1] has noticed that the spring, stream, pond, or whatever the source of the water-supply may have been, always appears to have a direct relation to a farmyard, so that we may fairly conclude that the germ of the village was a farm, and everything else about it the result

[1] *Berks, Bucks, and Oxon Archæological Journal,* vol. xxiii., p. 58. The writer is Mr. Llewellyn Treacher, F.G.S.

either of the natural development of the farm itself, or of institutions introduced from the outside, the water-supply, however, being for a long time the dominating factor.

The next requisite for a successful village was good soil, and the question naturally arises: How did the founders of our villages determine the nature and character of the soil? Were they obliged to cut down the trees that grew in the primæval forest in order to establish their settlements? It is true that the Saxons cleared away the forest trees, and called their villages *field*, such as Arborfield, Shinfield, etc., places where trees were *felled*. But a great part of the country must have been of an open park-like character; though the vegetation was wild, the beasts, the deer and oxen, were wild also, and these were browsing rather than grazing animals and would keep down the undergrowth in the woodlands. Doubtless many farms would be formed in good and bad situations, on good and bad land. Those not favourably placed would die a natural death, while those situate on good land would thrive and develop into villages. The villages are an excellent example of the survival of the fittest.

So our villages came into being during the Celtic period. The Neolithic folk had passed away or been absorbed by their conquerors. The Belgæ and other more warlike folk had imposed their rule on the peaceful agriculturists, developing into military leaders and chiefs, and in return for the services they exacted from them they kept order at home and defended the peaceful inhabitants from enemies abroad; and it was their inheritance into which the Romans entered when they conquered the country.

Perhaps there is no subject in connection with his own country of which the average Englishman knows less than the Roman occupation. A conquest by a terrible person who divided all Gaul into three parts, a great wall to keep out the Pictish tribes built by somebody else, he is not quite sure who, some very straight roads, and the fact that Roman remains, such as galleys and coins, are occasionally found in the island, pretty well sum up the conception of the average man. He has heard of Silchester, but has not thought it worth a visit, being, indeed, not at all sure where Silchester may be; he has a hazy notion that the Romans had something to do with the hot springs at Bath; and he may recollect having heard in some sermon that there was a British Church before the coming of Augustine. But it is extremely improbable that, if catechised on the subject, he will show any knowledge of the fact that the Roman era in Britain lasted rather longer than the period from Henry VI. to George V., and that for close upon four centuries England was as much a part of the Roman Empire as Italy itself.

On the whole, there is not much to wonder at in this popular ignorance. To the Roman, Britain was very insignificant and extremely provincial; and therefore it occupies no very large place in his literature, and most of his civilisation vanished with the inroads of the Anglo-Saxons. But the researches of industrious antiquaries during the last thirty years have added enormously to our knowledge of Roman Britain, and enable us to form some conception of the kind of life that was lived in this country when the Romans ruled, and especially in our own villages.

Their continuity is remarkable. When the Romans came and established their rule over Britain, they took over the control of the villages by means of a sort of peaceful penetration rather than by violent methods of conquest except in those parts of the country where vigorous opposition was encountered. In the gardens of old manor-houses, as at Childrey in Berkshire, Roman coins are often found, and in some cases coins of Cunobeline; and British coins of a rude type testify to the existence of pre-Roman occupation. The survival of Celtic names points to the same conclusion. Take for example the town of Hitchin, called in the Domesday Survey "Hiz," which is a Celtic word meaning "streams." There British sepulchral urns have been found, and also a Roman cemetery with a large number of urns and coins of Severus, Carausius, Constantine, and Allectus. All this shows that Hitchin was a British and a Roman settlement before it became a Saxon town. The same story can be traced in the village of Much Wymondley,[1] Litlington, Sandy, Meppershall, Pirton, and in many other places.

In many villages, Roman villas have been discovered, which are often fine houses which I will

[1] *The English Village Community*, by F. Seebohm, p. 430.

describe presently. The name "villa" is really a misnomer, as Mr. John Ward has pointed out in his work on *Roman Britain*. He says that "the villa was the Roman counterpart of the mediæval manor—the estate of a landed proprietor. It comprised not only his residence, but those of his *villicus* or bailiff and of his servile or semi-servile dependants, his farm buildings and granaries. The estate was the villa, the residence of the *dominus* or lord was the villa house."

These houses were usually spacious and comfortable, and many large and palatial. They abound in the south of England, and as far as Lincolnshire, but are scarce in the northern parts of the country which were not fully Romanised, and where the Legions had to protect the land from its northern neighbours. These southern homesteads show no evidences of defences. The country was peaceful; the Roman rule, here as in other lands, produced order and safety, and there was no need for the country gentlemen, who lived in the villages, to defend themselves from troublesome neighbours. It is usually stated that those who dwelt in the villas were Roman officials, foreigners from Rome or Gaul. But Mr. Ward thinks that these men resided chiefly in the towns, though some of the Roman villas, such as the Woodchester example, were doubtless the abodes of such officials. But these people were not very numerous, certainly not enough to inhabit all the villas that have been found or that remain to be discovered. These rural mansions were the seats of persons who occupied the position of country squires; they were usually natives, of British lineage, who during the long occupation of the Romans had adopted Roman tastes and acquired wealth from their broad acres, their crops and herds.

British agriculture was an important industry. It was a great wheat-growing country, and its corn wealth was one of the attractions which brought the Romans to our shores. It is on record that in the fourth century, when agriculture in the Rhenish countries failed or was interrupted by hordes of barbarians, the Huns of ancient days, the Emperor Julian arranged for the import of corn from Britain, and chartered 600 vessels to convey the supply to Rome. As in later times British sheep produced good wool, and this was woven into cloth by native industry and exported. An edict of the Emperor Diocletian records that British cloth was very famous, and was sent to Eastern countries.

In imagination we will excavate a Roman villa, such as doubtless stood in your village if it be an ancient one, or examine one that has already been disinterred. Roman villas are unlike any other dwellings that have been seen in Britain either before or since the Roman era. There are two types of these houses; one is called the corridor type and the other the basilican. Some years ago the Roman town of Silchester was thoroughly excavated, and the plans of numerous houses laid bare; and this great work has added notably to our knowledge of Roman Britain. These Silchester houses were not unlike the country houses, but being situate in a town their sites were restricted, and they could not expand themselves as the rural habitations, which were often on a large scale. The builder knew how to choose his site, and his favourite one was the sunny side of a gently sloping hill with a pleasant open prospect and near a spring of water or a running brook. The buildings were ranged around an open court, sometimes on three sides, or occasionally on four, forming a quadrangle like an Oxford College. Round the square ran a covered colonnaded walk or corridor which gave access to the numerous rooms. The roof of the corridor was supported by pillars. The foundations of the house were laid with stone or brick, and the walls were made by timber-framing, the interstices being filled with "wattle and daub," similar to the construction of many old cottages, farmhouses, and the "Magpies" of Cheshire. It is thought that most of these houses were only of one story, but at Silchester some traces of stairs were discovered. The rooms were numerous, but small, ranging from about twenty feet to as many as eighty. There were winter and summer quarters, the former being heated by hypocausts. Perhaps it is hardly necessary in these enlightened days to describe a hypocaust, but for the benefit of the uninitiated I may say that it consisted of a heated chamber beneath the floor of the room, which was supported by little pillars of brick or masonry and consisted of cement. A furnace projected outside into a yard or shed, and generated hot air which penetrated into the hypocaust and was carried into the rooms by vertical flue-tiles. In this way the Roman made himself warm and comfortable in the depth of our northern winter. The same method was adopted for heating the baths, which were usually a feature of every country house. These were similar to our Turkish baths, and included a cooling room, the *tepidarium*, *caldarium*, and sometimes a specially hot room called the *sudatorium*.

The windows of the house were glazed, and within it there were bright colours on the walls with delicate marbles and stuccoes of brilliant hues. The artist who decorated the walls copied nature as he saw it around him. Instead of the vine with clusters of grapes which adorn the walls of Italian villas, he used to copy the ears of corn growing in our British fields. Shrines and frescoes and statues decorated the interior; a fountain splashed water in the courtyard wherein bright flowers grew, and all the floors of the house had tessellated pavements, dearly loved by every Roman. Some floors were composed of simple red *tessellæ*, but in the principal rooms, frequented by the master and his family, there were produced by these variously coloured little cubes the old legends of the gods, Bacchus with his wild rout, Orpheus charming the animals with his lute, Apollo singing to his lyre, Venus loved by Mars, Neptune with a host of seamen, scollops and trumpets, Narcissus by the fountain, Jove and Ganymede, Leda and the Swan, wood-nymphs and naiads, satyrs and fauns, masks, hautboys, cornucopiæ, flowers, and baskets of golden fruit.

A fine Roman house was discovered some years ago near Winchcombe, in Gloucestershire, at Spoon-

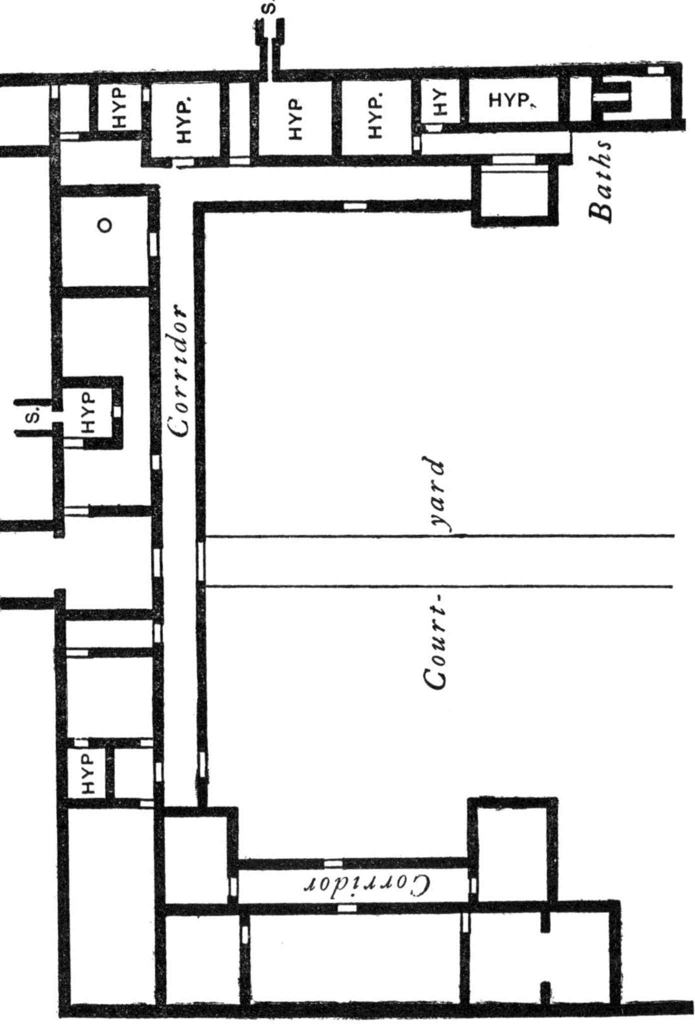

PLAN OF HOUSE AT SPOONLEY WOOD. (AFTER ROY)
(40 feet to 1 inch)
(From Ward's *Romano-British Buildings*)

ley Wood; of which a plan is shown. It is a good example of a medium-sized house reared in a fine situation. The plan speaks for itself and requires little description. As you will observe, it consists of a main range with two wings. In front there is a large courtyard with a wall completing its enclosure; in the centre of the wall was a gate and a paved path led to the front door. The word HYP in the plan denotes hypocaust. The length of the main range was 190 feet.

Around the house were stables, byres, mills, barns, granaries, and other outbuildings and houses for slaves and retainers. The remains of a barn have been discovered at the house I have just described. It must have resembled in size and plan one of those great mediæval barns such as Great Coxwell, and had a nave and aisles separated by two rows of timber posts. One of the largest of these villas is the notable one at Woodchester, which had two courtyards, and was a very sumptuous dwelling.

The basilical type of house was oblong in plan and resembled the Roman basilica or court of justice, and was not dissimilar to the barn-like structure attached to the Spoonley Wood villa. I have already compared the latter to a mediæval barn with its central nave and aisles. Rooms were formed by setting up partitions, and hypocausts were erected, and elaborate tessellated pavements were laid down. These houses are more primitive than the corridor type, and were probably inhabited by well-to-do farmers, or the *villicus*, or bailiff, of the master.

The Brading example forms part of the colony of buildings connected with the well-known country house or villa with its beautiful pavements which all visitors to the Isle of Wight admire so much.

In such houses as these even the Roman, accus-

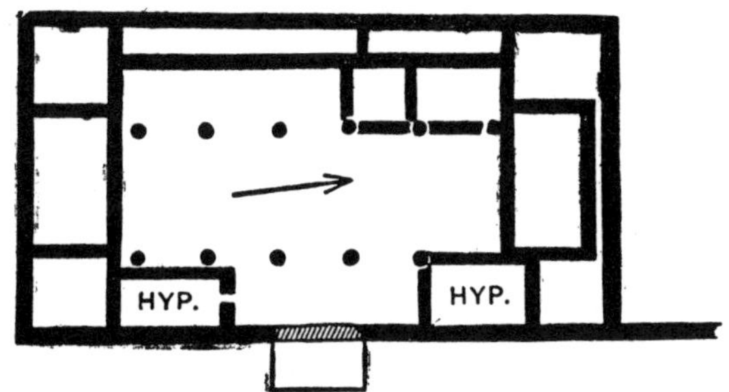

HOUSE AT CLANVILLE (40 FEET TO 1 INCH)

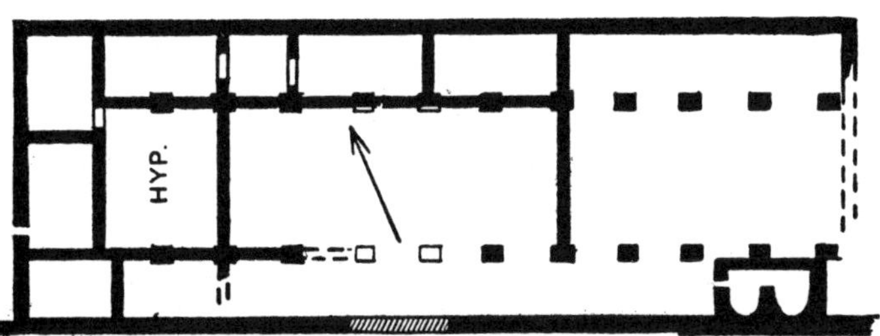

HOUSE AT BRADING (40 FEET TO 1 INCH)
(From Ward's *Roman Era*)

tomed to the sunny lands and blue skies of Italy, would not find himself altogether uncomfortable. But it may be safely conjectured, as I have stated, that some Briton who had raised himself and done good service to the ruling races sometimes dwelt therein. The veterans of the Legions, who were by no means always Romans, were a privileged class, and had grants of land in lieu of pay for their services to the Empire, just as it is proposed to reward our own gallant soldiers of to-day. These men, perhaps, held some of these rural abodes and lived as lords over their servile or semi-servile dependants. The life they lived in them must have been very pleasant. In the summer the quadrangle would be gay with calthæ, and the colonnade festooned with roses and helichryse. And when the long nights fell and winter cold set in, the slaves heaped higher the charcoal fires in the *præfurnium*, and the master sat in rooms far better warmed than many a country house is now, or sunned himself at midday in the sheltered quadrangle, or strolled in the warm side of the colonnade among the gay stuccoes and fluted columns. If he was a scholar perhaps he studied Virgil and gathered useful information from the Georgics with regard to his farming, and learned how best to grow wheat, the rotation of crops, the picking of grain, the drainage of land, the pasturing of sheep, the cleaning of the young crop from noxious weeds, bee-keeping and bird-scaring. He would discover the most approved methods of cultivating barley, flax, beans, vetches, and lentils; and delight in the picture of the winter scenes in sunny Italy which were not unlike those on his own farm, the ploughman sharpening the blunted share, the slaves harvesting the apples, the shepherd marking his sheep, the housewife busy with her bread-oven, and the maids carding wool. He would learn how to rear and breed stock, and perhaps smile with satisfaction when he compared his own heifers with the poet's description of a beast with an ugly head, long neck, dewlaps extending to the legs, though he might like to add to his stables such a mettled steed with neck raised high, head little and slender, barrel short, back plump, chest swelling, with brawny muscle and the solid horn of the hoof. All this and much more he would learn from Virgil's writings; and then he might turn to Pliny and discover some ideas of scientific farming, and learn about his own people; that the people of Kent were the most civilised of all the British tribes, and that their system of agriculture included the marling of land. With such instructors the Romanised British lord would not fail to improve his farming methods and eradicate his barbarous and primitive notions about cultivating his land.

But the Villa was not the only house in the village, and the cottages and the general aspect of the hamlet remain to be described. In addition to the *villa urbana*, the residence of the proprietor, there was the *villa rustica*, where his *villicus*, or bailiff, and other farm dependants lived. These corresponded to our modern manor-house and what we call the home-farm. This was in the form of a basilica with nave and aisles, and with rooms for the family and servants at each end. These houses have been compared with the early Saxon farm-houses, and it has been conjectured that their use was similar. On either side of the central nave there would be stalls for horses and oxen, and above these storage for hay and corn. The farm-hands would sleep in these lofts, and a fire on a hearth would keep them warm at night, the smoke ascending to the roof and finding its way out through holes. In some of these Roman farmhouses there are evidences of considerable attempts at comfort. There were hypocausts, as at Brading and Mansfield Woodhouse, and a considerable number of rooms partitioned off from the central nave; and mosaic pavements, wall-plaster and window-glass have been sometimes found, showing a degree of luxury that was wanting in many of these dwellings.

In addition to these types of houses there were the dwellings of the humbler folk—the labourers and slaves. As I have said, some of these probably dwelt in the lofts over the cattle stalls; but cottages have been discovered. Antiquaries owe much to the careful exploration of a village site on Woodcuts Common in Cranbourne Chase by General Pitt Rivers; but owing to the slight foundations of the houses not very reliable results could be obtained. He discovered that these dwellings were built of wattles and daub, and coated with lime and mould, mixed in some cases with small fragments of flint. They were roofed with stone or red clay roofing tiles. However, the British in the early period of the Roman occupation had not abandoned their pit-dwellings, which, when deserted as living abodes, were used as cellars or store-pits for the houses.

As we roam through Britain in the Roman period examining its towns and villages, we discover abundant evidence of a widely diffused culture among Britons as among Romans during at least the last half of the Roman occupation—a culture which in certain respects far more nearly resembles that of modern times, than in almost any of the intervening period. The pottery, tools, household ware, jewellery, ornaments, toys, which have been found in abundance, are not greatly inferior to those of the same date discovered in Italy. Plainly during the four and a half centuries of their occupation they brought the country to a high state of civilisation. They constructed a splendid system of roads. Of course these do not always follow an undeviating straight line as the popular idea imagines; but what has given rise to the superstition is the fact that the Roman engineers were apt to make each section a straight line. Very few of the bridges which are supposed to be Roman are really so, but, on the other hand, many fords which are still in use are of undoubted Roman work. A Roman ford was simply a submerged portion of the road, only it was constructed with special care. In 1820 there was one running across the Trent near Lincoln, which was removed as being a hindrance to navigation. It was a pavement of large squared stones held in place by two rows of piles, and that bit of Roman work had resisted the rush and scour of the Trent for at least 1,600 years.

The system of posting-stations was at least equal to that which served the old mail-coaches. From Dover to the Wall life and property were as vigilantly guarded as they are to-day. They built many towns, and these were carefully planned and laid out, mostly it would seem on the plan which finds so much favour in modern America, whereby the streets cut one another at right angles, forming *insulæ*, but the houses were kept well apart, and town gardens were encouraged.

Further, they rendered the country secure from the Picts, spending money and labour without stint for the great northern walls occupying all the strategical positions with camps and forts. Of all the Roman remains in Britain none approaches in interest the two stupendous Walls which we owe to the genius of Agricola. The Northern Wall runs from the Forth to the Clyde, and the Southern, now generally known as "the" Roman Wall, from Newcastle to Carlisle. Probably the idea was to create a sort of buffer State between the two Walls; and we know that the Northern fortification was constantly manned from the troops stationed along the Southern line. Hadrian, however, found it impossible or unwise to maintain the forward policy of Agricola, and the Northern Wall was finally abandoned, the line from the Tyne to the Solway being adopted as the real frontier of the Roman Empire. This, which is called the Wall of Hadrian, is a solid structure of stone, and is seventy-three and a half miles in length. It was about ten feet thick, and the ditch appears to average about fifteen feet deep and thirty-six feet wide. Roughly speaking, there was a small fort at every mile, and a garrison station at every four miles. All were connected by a magnificent military road, and we may say that as a piece of military engineering the Roman Wall is unsurpassed in Europe even to-day. I may add that the *graffiti* which are gradually being collected from various parts of this wonderful fortification show how amazingly cosmopolitan were the troops which held it. There must have been many brown and some black men among the legionaries who garrisoned the Wall. It is a curious illustration of the difficulty attending the investigation of the Roman period in Britain that though we know it was Agricola who chose the line, we do not know even now whether it was Hadrian or Severus who really built the Wall.

Moreover, they guarded the sea against raiders and invaders who wrought such havoc after their departure. They promoted trade. I have already mentioned the large amount of wheat that was grown and exported, so that Britain became one of the chief granaries of the Empire, and the good cloth that was manufactured; mining for coal, lead, tin, and copper, were national industries; pottery, glass, and fine enamels, were among the productions of the people, and the iron works seem to have been immense. The unguarded state of the country villas, as I have already mentioned, tells its own tale of internal peace, and if Britain did not attain the wealth and refinement of Italy, it nevertheless appears to have been an agreeable place to live in, and its insular position saved it from some of the political troubles which fell upon the Continental parts of the Empire during the same period.

There is, of course, a reverse side of which we get hints in the story of Boadicea and in the complaint of the monk, Gildas. At certain periods taxation was oppressive, and compulsory military service abroad or in the fleet was felt to be a gross tyranny by the British. It is suggested that the British squires, the inhabitants of the rich villas, reduced the peasantry to slavery, and that their great estates ruined the country and greatly reduced its population as the *latifundia* are said to have done in Italy. The evidence of this, however, is very scanty, and equally so the evidence for another complaint, made on the authority of Gildas, that the *pax Romana* made the people effeminate and deprived them of their power of self-defence Anyhow, they did for two hundred years make a vigorous defence against both Picts and English invaders after the withdrawal of the Roman legions. The scenes of slaughter and destruction in which the Roman civilisation went down may be imagined from the tales of the later chroniclers, but it was a prolonged death-throe, not a sudden extinction as is usually supposed. For centuries later the ruins of towns and villas must have been a familiar picture on the countryside, and the Anglo-Saxon builders no doubt learnt their art from their Roman predecessors. There was a rumour in the learned world not long ago that a German scholar had discovered an Anglo-Saxon poem which was in all probability a lament over the ruins of the Roman city of Bath, but that may be as spurious as Herr Bode's Leonardo da Vinci's bust.

As regards religion the Romans brought their gods with them and then cheerfully tacked on the Roman Pantheon the native deities of Britain and others imported from abroad. We find their names on numerous altars in all parts of the country. And with the Romans came Christianity. Church history tells us how it came, and legends attribute its introduction to St. Paul, or St. Peter, or Joseph of Arimathea; but these stories may be disregarded. Christian soldiers of the Legions, merchants from Gaul, traders and travellers, would tell the Gospel story to the inhabitants of our island, and priests would follow and confirm their faith. It seems strange that archæology and the diligent search among Roman relics have yielded few evidences of Christianity in Britain. There is the little church at Silchester, and another at Caerwent. The Silchester Church was excavated by the Society of Antiquaries, but it is now again covered by earth. It is very similar in form to the early churches in Italy. The orientation is different from that used after the reign of Constantine, the altar being at the west end. The officiating priest stood behind the altar facing the congregation and looking towards the east at the time of the celebration of Holy Communion. A plan of the church is shown with a conjectural restoration. There is an apse at the west end, and the building is divided by two rows of columns into a nave and two aisles. The nave had probably an ambo or reading-desk, and was mainly used by the clergy; one aisle was for the women, the other for the men. Across the eastern end was the narthex or porch, where the catechumens stood and watched the service through the three open doors. Outside the narthex was the atrium, an open court, having in the centre the

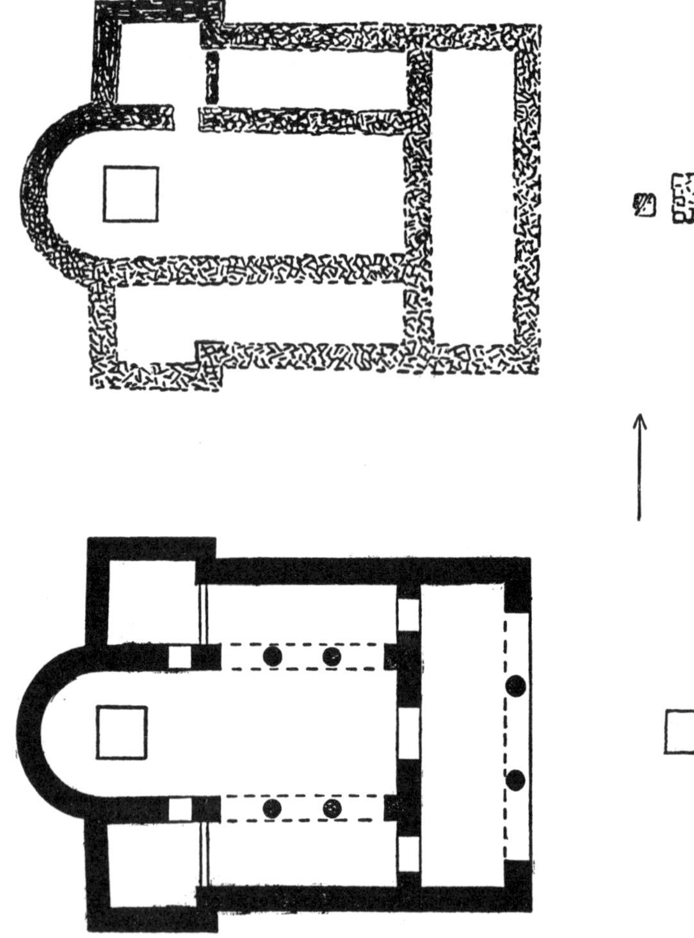

PLAN OF CHURCH AT SILCHESTER AND CONJECTURAL RESTORATION
(15 feet to 1 inch)
(From Ward's *Romano-British Buildings*)

labrum, or laver, where the people washed their hands and faces before entering the church.

Bede states that St. Martin's at Canterbury was built when the Romans were in the island, and the churches of Reculver, Dover Castle, Lyminge and part of Bosham are said to be of Roman origin. A few instances of the use of the XP monogram, the first letters of Christ, engraved on various objects, and some Christian inscriptions on tombs, are all the evidence that archæology can furnish. Perhaps the early Romano-British Christians were poor, and could not afford to possess Christian emblems engraved on ornaments, but there is plenty of evidence of the existence of the British Church. There were many martyrs during the Diocletian persecution, and the little church at Silchester probably arose when the edict of toleration was issued. At the beginning of the third century Tertullian testifies that parts of Britain were subject to Christ, and several other Fathers of the Church—Athanasius, Chrysostom, Hilary of Poitiers, and Jerome—speak highly of British faith and discipline. The Bishops of London, York, and Caerleon, attended Church Councils at Arles, Sardica, and Ariminium; and when the Saxons came with fire and sword into the island and drove the Britons westward, they took with them their religion and joined their Celtic brethren in Wales and Cornwall, where Christianity flourished and the Church prospered during the darkness of Anglo-Saxon England.

But it is quite possible that, as Mr. Ward in his book on *The Roman Era in Britain* conjectures, "the Faith may have survived the English Conquest to a greater extent than is commonly supposed, and that many of our existing churches of most ancient foundation had a Roman origin."

As at Rome, where a Christian congregation used to assemble for worship in the house of one of its leading members—St. Paul sends greetings to a certain lady and "the Church that is in her house"—so here in Britain the Christian squire would set apart a room for his family and dependants to hold their religious services, which would be taken by a chaplain or missionary-priest. Such is, in brief, a sketch of village life in Britain during the Roman period, and it may be conjectured that it was not an undesirable country to live in, at least for those who dwelt in the villas. The lot of the slaves or semi-servile population might not be always happy. It depended upon the will of the lord of the villa, and with a good master the slaves would not fare ill. At Colchester there is a statue of a Roman centurion that was erected by two grateful freemen. We hear of one slave complaining because he was struck and beaten when he was helping the soldiers to make roads. Sometimes on account of the heavy tribute demanded all the people in a village would surrender their liberty to the dominus, in order to escape payment.

As we proceed we shall see the development of the villa into the Norman manor, and the close resemblance between the two. I have not touched upon the Tribal system, which prevailed in Western Britain, with its peculiar features, but, perforce, I must leave that alone, or this chapter would never end, and we must seek "fresh woods and pastures new."

The Centurion Monument,
Colchester

CHAPTER VI

THE SAXON VILLAGE

The withdrawal of the Romans—The Saxon Conquest—Bede's account—Destruction of villas—Family settlements—Nomenclature—English villages—Agriculture—Lammas lands—Free communities—Land tenures—The lord's house—Geburs—Cottiers—Slaves—Socmen—Village trades and officials—The church—Saxon relics.

THE legend that we find in our old history books that the British, enfeebled by Roman luxury, after the departure of the Legions fell an easy prey to the people who for convenience' sake we call the Anglo-Saxons, is entirely mythical. It must be remembered that with the Legions were withdrawn some of the best fighting blood in the Roman armies, the British young men who had been called to the standards, and followed them to fight against the German barbarians who were threatening the existence of the Empire. This process began in the early years of the fifth century, but the life of the villages, at least those in the southern part of the country, far removed from the troublesome Pictish tribes in the north, went on in much the same manner as before. Season succeeded season; crops were sown and reaped; golden apples were gathered in the orchards; but there were ominous signs of coming trouble. Stories are told by the later chroniclers of the British folk begging the Legionaries not to leave them, but these tales are probably imaginary. However, there was cause for anxiety. The villagers had heard rumours of certain wild pirates who came from the Eastand who pillaged and slew, with "frightfulness" that has recently been imitated, the inhabitants who dwelt along the coast, even before the Romans had left. Some of their lads had been summoned to serve in the ships of the Roman officer, the Count of the Saxon Shore, and had brought back sad news of the barbarous manners of the invaders. Who were these peoples? They came in their long ships from the lands bordering on the sea-coasts extending from the mouth of the Rhine to the Baltic, Angles, Saxons, Jutes, and the rest, fierce warriors to a man, pagan, worshippers of Thor and Woden, the German gods of whom we have heard much lately, bloodthirsty and savage. During the century and a half which followed the departure of the Romans they came, and the sight of their vessels struck terror into the hearts of those who lived along the coast in towns and villages which after many a gallant defence fell into their power, and they were masters of the bays and harbours from the mouth of the Humber to Southampton Water, occupying the adjacent lands. The Anglo-Saxon Chronicle states: "A.D. 491. This year Ælla and Cissa besieged Andredscester and slew all that dwelt therein, so that not a single Briton was there left." This was the old Roman fortress of Anderida, now called Pevensey; and the tragedy that happened there was doubtless repeated in many other places.

With a preacher's love of moralising, Bede attributes the plight of the Britons to their wickedness, their cruelty, hatred of truth and love of falsehood, bred of luxury, while their clergy were addicted to drunkenness, animosity, litigiousness, contention, and other such crimes, and the casting off the light yoke of Christ. They were troubled with a severe plague, and their foolish agreement to invite the Saxons to aid them against the Picts was the cause of their undoing, a punishment sent by our Lord upon them for their wicked deeds. The Venerable Bede's History is the most wonderful heritage of the English people. No other nation in Europe possesses such a treasure; but though he is a sure guide to the events that occurred in his own time, his narrative of those that preceded his own period, depending upon the stories that were transmitted to him from an earlier age, is not always to be depended upon. The Jutes, Frisians, Angles, and Saxons required no invitation to come into Britain. It is now generally understood that they acquired their settlement in this country rather by a long course of predatory inroads than in the rapid and somewhat dramatic manner related by Bede.

But all that I have recorded was only preparatory to the Conquest of Britain and the making of England. It is beyond my purpose to describe the course of that conquest, to discuss the question propounded by my friend, the late Sir Laurence Gomme, as to whether London was captured by the Angles, or their campaign in the conquest of the Thames Valley, as told by another friend, Major

Godsal, who ridicules the idea of the "long boat" theory, and maintains that the campaign that led mainly to the complete conquest of the country was a masterpiece of military strategy, of which as a soldier he is a better judge than we ordinary antiquaries. I have to concern myself with English village life, and must pass by such inviting themes.

As I have said, for many years the quietude of country life was undisturbed, but the villagers had a rude awakening. The British fought hard against the ever-advancing foe. They won; they lost; but the Anglo-Saxon hordes, whether coming from the south or the east, always won their way in the end. And what happened to the villagers? Bede records:

> They plundered all the neighbouring cities and country spread the conflagration from the Eastern to the Western Sea, without any opposition, and covered almost every part of the devoted island. Public as well as private structures were overturned; the priests were everywhere slain before the altars; the prelates and the people, without any respect of persons, were destroyed with fire and sword; nor was there any to bury those who had been thus cruelly slaughtered. Some of the miserable remainder, being taken in the mountains, were butchered in heaps. Others spent with hunger came forth and submitted themselves to the enemy for food, being destined to undergo perpetual servitude, if they were not killed upon the spot. Some with sorrowful hearts fled beyond the seas. Others, continuing in their own country, led a miserable life among the woods, rocks, and mountains, with scarcely enough food to support life, and expecting every moment to be their last.

Such is Bede's narrative, but it is a little fanciful. It is questionable whether the destruction was so great. We look at Silchester, a city entirely in ruins, save its protecting walls, with grass fields covering the remains of houses, basilica, baths, temples; surely this must be the work of devastating hordes. However, authorities tell us that there are no signs of any sudden overthrow of the city, that its decay was quite gradual. It is possible that its Romano-British inhabitants may have fled, as so many did before the invaders' approach, and found a refuge in Wales or Cornwall. But there is reason for the belief that, as the English (as we may begin to call them) advanced westward, they abandoned their ferocity. The western towns of Bath, Gloucester, and Cirencester survived, and doubtless many a humble village was spared. Perhaps they were influenced by their beauty, by the rich cornlands and evidences of civilised life. They feared no longer any organised opposition; and so they took over the villages, which they greatly preferred to the towns, established their village communities, and made slaves of the Britons who remained.

The beautiful villas shared a common fate. The English liked not these luxurious abodes. Their semi-savage nature revolted from the exhibition of a culture they could not understand. So the torch was applied to the buildings and the timber structures soon blazed away and became a heap of ruins. As an accomplished writer[1] has said:

> So it was all through the land, and so the scarred heaps of débris marked the sites of the old villas on their sunny southern slopes, until the baths were choked, and the roofs of the hypocausts fell in, and the grass came up through

[1] Mr. J. Meade Falkner, *A History of Oxfordshire.*

the tessellæ, and spread a cloak over all, and finally the plough levelled even the mounds, the last memorial of the happy homes that had passed away. Something of the same kind may be seen on the north coast of Africa to-day, where in the waste the wrecks of Rome—the houses lining the narrow streets, the bases of colonnaded pillars, and even the triumphal arch—still stand gaunt, shattered, and alone.

Having possessed themselves of the soil the English set to work to colonise the conquered country. In their warfare they kept together in tribes and families. Hence in their settlement they followed the same order, when founding their village communities. In the names of places we often notice the suffix *ing*, meaning *sons of*. This denotes that the village was first occupied by the clan of some chieftain, whose name is compounded with this syllable *ing*. Thus the Uffingas, the children of Offa, formed a settlement at Uffinggaston, or Uffington: the Readingas, or sons of Rede, settled at Reading; the Billings at Billinge and Billingham; the Wokings or Hôcings, sons of Hôç, at Woking and Wokingham. The Billings and Wokings first settled at Billinge and Woking; and then like bees they swarmed, and started another hive of industry at Billingham and Wokingham.

There are many other family settlements that are revealed to us by this patronymic *ing*. At Ardington, in Berkshire, the Ardings, the royal race of the Vandals, settled; the Frankish Walsings at Walsingham; the Halsings at Helsington; the Brentings at Brentingley; the Danish Seyldings at Skelding; the Thurings at Thorington; and many other examples might be quoted.

These people entered into the possession of the Romano-British villages and "called the lands after their own names." Occasionally a British name remains, but seldom with regard to places, although such natural features as rivers and hills were permitted to retain their former names. The science and study of place-names have progressed enormously during recent years, and old notions and weird guesses that satisfied our fathers have been altogether abandoned. Much history can be learned from them, and amongst other facts we gather from the prevalence of Saxon words the knowledge of the complete conquest of the greater part of the country by these invaders. The meaning of these Saxon terminations is now so well known that I am almost afraid of repeating an oft-told tale. But for the benefit of the uninitiated I may state that a word ending in *field* denotes a forest clearing where trees were *felled* by the axes of the settlers. Thus we have Bradfield, or the "broad field"; Englefield, "the field of the Angles"; Fyfield, formerly "five-fields," or "five hides," "as it was anciently designated; Ganfield, "the field of Gamel." Stratfield is the field near the street or Roman road, thus preserving the memory of the work of the Romans. No Saxon termination is so common as *ham*, which has two significations, one answering to the Anglo-Saxon *hām*, meaning "home," and the other to *hamm*, an enclosure, whence the modern English phrase *to hem in* is derived. It is not always possible to determine to which class a given example belongs. My own village, Barkham, formerly spelt

Beorcham or Berchcham, signifies "birch-home" or the home near a birch-tree. The large number of names ending in *ham* testifies to the English love of their homes. As an illustration of the other meaning of *ham* I may mention Wittenham, which signifies the enclosure of a gentleman named Witta.

The suffix *Bergh* or *Berh* means a hill; *bourn* or *borne* a stream; *bury*, a borough; *combe*, a hollow on the flank of a hill, is a relic of Celtic nomenclature which was retained by the Anglo-Saxons. *Cot* is naturally a cottage or small house. *Cross* is a curious word; the pagan conquerors had no use for such a word. It is really a Celtic word adapted from the Latin *crucem*. *Don* or *Down* means a hill and is not to be confused with *ton*, one of the commonest Saxon suffixes, a town, homestead, or village, surrounded by a protecting palisade. *Ey* means an island. Near Oxford there is a village called Hinksey, or "Hengest's isle," thus preserving the name of some notable chief. *Hay* signifies a fence; *hithe*, a landing-place; *holt* and *hurst*, a wood; *ley*, a field; *low*, a burial-mound. We have a curious name in Berkshire, Inkpen, which seems to have some connection with authorship. I used to think that *pen* signified a hill. We have the Pennine Range, Pendle Hill; but Professor Skeat states that when it occurs as a suffix it means a pen for cattle, and that Inkpen is really Inga's pen or sheepfold. There are some other terminations with which I need not trouble you. It is significant, however, that most of the names in Southern England and in the Midlands are Saxon, and this demonstrates the complete conquest and occupation by the conquerors of these districts. The names in East Anglia and in the North denote the presence of other conquering peoples, the Danes. All place-names ending in *by* proclaim their presence, while in Wales and in the West Country the continued use of Celtic names shows that these districts were the havens of rest of the dispossessed Romano-British people.

It is possible to realise the conditions of life in an English village when the Anglo-Saxons had settled down in the country, and made themselves at home in the places they had won by their swords and battle-axes The village consisted of a number of families, usually about thirty, and the land was divided regularly into three portions. There was the village itself, in which the people lived in rude houses built of wood or rough stone-work. Around the village were a few small enclosures, or grass yards, for rearing calves and baiting farm stock; this was the common farmstead. Around this was the arable land, where the villagers grew their corn, wheat, oats, and rye, beans and barley; and around this the common meadows, or pasture land, held by the whole community, so that each family could turn their cattle into it, subject to the regulations of an officer elected by the people, whose duty it was to see that no one trespassed on the rights of his neighbours, or turned too many cattle into this common pasture. Around the whole colony lay the woods and uncultivated land, which was left in its natural state, where the people cut their timber and fuel, and pastured their pigs in the glades of the forest.

The cultivated land was divided into three large fields, each field being ploughed into narrow strips, these being separated by unploughed belts of grass-land usually called baulks, either side baulks if they ran parallel with the furrows, or headland baulks when running across the end of the furrows. The groups of strips were called furlongs—*i.e.*, "furrow-longs" —or "shots." In different parts of the country these divisions of land had various other names

EARLY ANGLO-SAXON PLOUGHING
(From Hone's *Manor and Manorial Records*)

which need not be mentioned here. It is interesting to note how the communal system was carried out in all the agricultural arrangements of the village. To each freeman was assigned his own family lots, which were cultivated by the members of his household. These lots were scattered in various parts of the fields, so that the good land might not all be assigned to a few privileged mortals, while bad land was left to the unfortunate members of the community. Though they were freemen they were not allowed to follow their own wills and inclinations. They knew that if the same sort of crop was grown upon the same soil year after year, they would reap a poor harvest; so the rotation of crops was rigidly enforced, and every man was obliged to sow the same crop as his neighbour. They knew also that the soil becomes exhausted if it be forced to bear too often. So they made a rule that each field should lie fallow once in three years. When the corn was reaped and the harvest gathered in, the arable fields were all thrown open for grazing. The same plan was adopted with the meadow or pasture land. This was divided into strips, and every head of a family had the right of drawing lots for the privilege of mowing and carrying the hay. After the hay harvest had been gathered in, the land became common property again.

We have still remains of this ancient field system. In many parishes there are still fields that are termed "lot meadows," or "Lammas lands," Lammas Day—the first day of August according to the old calendar, the 12th of our modern one—being the day when the pasture meadows were thrown open for the common use of the community. The name "Lammas" is derived from "Loaf-mass," when a loaf made from the first ripe corn was offered in the service of Holy Communion. The arable land, when the harvest had been gathered in, was thrown open at some later date, and not on Lammas Day, as some writers have stated.

In the *Laws of King Ine* there is a realistic description of a ceorle's grass-tun or meadow:

> If ceorls have common meadow or other land divided into strips to fence, and some have fenced their strip, and

some have not, and stray cattle eat their common acres or grass, let those go who own the gap, and compensate the others who have fenced their strip.

A very wise provision! And this was enacted in the seventh century in the old Wessex kingdom, showing clearly that the common open field system was then in vogue, the arable land being divided into acres and the meadows into doles, an arrangement that dates back to the earliest Saxon times.

How far the village was free has been much disputed. There have been many investigators, both in England and abroad, but they have not succeeded in fixing upon a unanimous opinion. There is the mark theory, advocated by Kemble, which states that all the land was held in common by different communities of settlers, each of which dwelt in and cultivated its own settlement, that was separated from its neighbours by a mark or boundary. Each village was free, only bound by the laws and rules established for the benefit of the community. It was a democracy; but for some reason, perhaps on account of military necessity for the sake of protection, the community took to itself a leader, commander, or lord, to act as its chief, and to seek in return certain services to be rendered by the men of the village who would thus become his tenants and servants. In his book on the *English Village Community* Mr. Seebohm points out that the English village community was the lineal descendant of the Roman villa and was always servile The conclusion at which most leading authorities have arrived is that the lord, or thane, or ruler, was imposed upon the original free community, and I desire to quote Professor Vinogradoff's opinion. He writes:

> The communal organisation of the peasantry is more ancient and more deeply laid than the manorial order. Even the feudal period shows everywhere traces of a peasant class living and working in economically self-dependent communities under the loose authority of a lord whose claims may proceed from political causes and affect the semblance of ownership, but do not give rise to the manorial connexion between estate and village.

But a darkness hangs over the fifth century, and it is difficult to pierce it. There may have been some independent communities, and in Wales where the tribal system existed there seems to have been a large amount of independence; but when the clouds disperse over English land we find that each village had its lord or thane, answering to the squire of to-day. As in modern times there are dukes and earls and lords with large estates with many villages upon them, so in Saxon days there were the *thani regis*, who served the king in Court, or in the management of State affairs; the *thani mediocres*, who held their titles and estates by inheritance, and corresponded to the lords of the manor of later times; and the *thani minores*, to which rank men who could not claim noble birth—successful merchants and the like—could attain by the acquisition of sufficient landed property. The king himself kept in his own hands many estates and villages, and in theory all the land in his kingdom, whether it was Wessex or Sussex or East Anglia or Mercia, belonged to him; but he made grants to his faithful thanes, and such lands were called bok-land or book-land. For the good of his soul or in repentance for his sins, when Christianity had dethroned the pagan worship of Odin and Thor, he used to make grants of lands to bishops and monasteries, and the Church became possessed of many villages.

The tenures by which these various owners held their lands are strange and curious, and were sometimes framed with some sense of humour. The person who arranged that a man should hold his lands by the service of holding the king's head when he crossed the seas was not lacking in humour in fixing upon that disagreeable duty. Usually the thane was required to provide food for the king and his retinue, not omitting his horses and hounds and hawks, when he passed through the village, or the more picturesque duty of presenting a rose on a certain day. Later on these tenures increased and multiplied. To hold the stirrup of the king when he mounted his horse at Carlisle Castle, to carry a hawk for His Majesty, to present him with a grey hood or cap, to blow horns, count the king's chessmen and put them into a bag when the king had finished the game—these are only a fraction of many instances of regal ingenuity.[1]

The most practical duties which the owner had to perform were to bear arms when called upon for the king's service in war, to repair fortresses, and to keep bridges in good repair. In feudal times this was called the *trinoda necessitas*. The Saxon

[1] Cf. *Old English Customs*, by P. H. Ditchfield, pp. 300-306.

gentleman had, therefore, many obligations to perform for his lord the king. He lived in a low, irregular, one-storied house in the centre of the village, the principal chamber being a hall in the centre of the building with the kitchen on one side, and, when he became a Christian, a chapel on the other. It was built of unplaned wood with pillars composed of oak-trees, the roots of which were placed upward so as to form the rafters of the roof. For purposes of defence the house was usually built in the form of a quadrangle, having a court in the centre, and all the windows looked into the courtyard. Mr. Baring-Gould in *Old Country Life* mentions some West Country houses that still follow that arrangement. An additional defence was supplied by a deep ditch or moat with a palisade composed of pointed planks on the side remote from the house.

The hall was the principal chamber in the building, and this traditional arrangement of a country house remained for centuries, though the Saxon thane's dwelling was far more rude and rough than those of his successors. It was long and wide and low, with a roof composed of rough-hewn beams. A fire burned in the centre of the hall, and the smoke blackened the timbers of the unceiled roof, hung as a cloud over the assembled guests, and finally made its escape through a hole in the roof. No planks or tiles covered the earthen floor that was strewn with reeds, save at the end where the thane and his family had their meals on a raised dais. Unplaned planks laid on trestles were brought in for the tables of the servants and housecarles. This arrangement lasted until Shakespeare's time, who makes Capulet in *Romeo and Juliet,* cry out:

> A hall! A hall! Give room to foot it, girls,
> More light, ye knaves; and turn the tables up,
> And quench the fire, the room is grown too hot.

The housecarles and servants, both men and women, separated by the arras, slept in the hall on straw, the lord's family having separate sleeping-apartments. The roof was thatched with reeds or rushes, and was seldom weatherproof, and the winds and gales blew through the crevices of the walls and provided ventilation. They were hardy folk or the draughts would have slain them, in spite of rich hangings on the walls. Sheepskin rugs were their only coverlets. An illustration of a thane's house appears in the Harleian MSS. No. 603, where the lord and lady are represented as engaged in almsgiving: the lady is earning her true title, that of "loaf-giver," from which her name "lady" is derived.

Arms and armour and implements of husbandry hung on the walls of the hall. The seats consisted of benches called "mead-settles" arranged along the sides of the apartment, where the Saxons sat drinking their favourite beverage, mead, or sweetened beer, out of the horns presented to them by the waiting damsels. As we know from Bede's account of the "morning star of English poetry," Cædmon, they used to sing songs, passing round the harp, each one singing in turn. Bards and gleemen were ever welcome guests, who used to delight the company by their songs and stories of the gallant deeds of their ancestors, the weird legends of their gods, Woden and Thor, their Viking lays and Norse sagas, and sometimes acrobats and dancers astonished them with their strange postures.

Around the lord's house were grouped the dwellings of the villagers, of whom there were several classes. I have mentioned the ceorl, or husbandman, a wide term embracing the lower class of

SWINEHERDS AND SWINE
(From Hone's *Manor and Manorial Records*)

freemen and all above the slaves. Next to the lord was the *gebur*, or owner of a yard-land, a bundle of thirty strips in the open fields, with two oxen in the common plough of eight oxen. In return for his holding he had to work three days a week for the lord with additional occasional services. Next in order came the *cottiers*, who were called later on in Norman times *bordarii* (a word derived from *bord*, a cottage). They had a holding of a few scattered strips in the open fields. In the *Rectitudines*, a book of rules of the tenth century, the work of a cottier is thus described:

He shall do what on the land is fixed; on some he shall, each Monday in the year, work for his lord and three days a week in harvest; he ought to have five acres in his holding; he pays hearth penny on Holy Thursday and Kirkshot at Martinmas.

Lastly, there were the *theows*, or slaves, who could be bought or sold in the market and exported to foreign lands. The price of a slave was one pound, equivalent to £2 16s. 3d. of our currency. Some of these were born in thraldom, and others were known to sell themselves into slavery on account of poverty and want.

Listen to the piteous complaint of one of this class recorded in a dialogue of Ælfric of the tenth century:

"What doest thou, ploughman? How dost thou do thy work?"

"Oh, my lord, hard do I work. I go out at daybreak, driving the oxen to the field, and I yoke them to the plough. Nor is it ever so hard that I dare loiter at home, for fear of my lord, but the oxen yoked, and the ploughshare and the coulter fastened to the plough, every day I must plough a full acre or more."

"Hast thou any comrade?"

"I have a boy driving the oxen with an iron goad, who also is hoarse with cold and shouting."

"What more dost thou in the day?"

"Verily then I do more. I must fill the bin of the oxen with hay, and water them, and carry out the dung. Ha! Ha! Hard work it is! because *I am not free.*"

Those last words convey the secret of his unhappiness. His work was not harder than that of a modern carter; but servitude galled his spirit and made his work intolerable. Let us hope that his lord was a kind-hearted man, and gave him his freedom. Frequently men were released from slavery, and later on the Church did good service in rescuing these unhappy people from bondage. When a man sold himself into slavery he laid aside his sword and lance, the symbols of the free, and took up the bill and the goad, the implements of bondage, falling on his knees before his lord, and placing his head under the hands of his master in token of submission. There was yet another class in the early English community. These were the *socmen*, a class which was called into being by the necessity of war. England was not a very peaceable country in the days of the Heptarchy or when Danish hordes invaded the land, and disputes between rival kingdoms were frequent and battles plentiful. Kings required armies of men who could fight, and every earl or thane had to furnish them. Hence, there was attached to every lord's estate a number of men with a supply of arms, who performed some of the agricultural duties on the home-farm, and were called socmen, especially in East Anglia, part of their duty being to attend the "soc" or "soke"—the lord's court of justice. But their principal obligation was to fight when required to do so by their lord. They were free tenants, and correspond to our yeomen who, by their independence, have stamped with peculiar features both our constitution and our national character. Their good name remains. English yeomen have done good service to their country, and never greater than in the recent Great War. The yeoman owns the farm he tills, and many suffered and had to sell their land during the long period of agricultural depression. Now that farming is reviving, we hope they may regain their lost position and preserve their good name.

Each village community was self-supporting. They were somewhat isolated,[1] and could not supply their needs from neighbouring towns. Every village had its own *faber*, or "harmonious black-

SHEPHERDS AND FLOCK
(From Hone's *Manor and Manorial Records*)

smith," a very indispensable person, and the carpenter who repaired the ploughs and put together the wooden framework of the houses, and in return for his work had a small holding among the tenants free from ordinary or boon work. There was the *pounder* who looked after the repair of the fences and impounded stray cattle; the *cementarius*, or stonemason; the *custos apium*, or bee-keeper, an important person, as much honey was needed to make the sweetened ale, or mead, which the villagers

[1] Cf. *Village Community*, by Sir Laurence Gomme, p. 159.

loved to imbibe; and the steward, or *prepositus*, who acted on behalf of the lord, looked after the interests of the tenants, and took care that they rendered their legal services. Each village brewed its own ale, provided itself with meat, baked its own bread, ground its own flour, grew flax for its linen, and caught the deer, hares, and rabbits in the surrounding woods.

They ought to have been very happy places, these Saxon villages, but the life was hard. The system of agriculture was wasteful and unproductive. There were frequent famines. The houses were poor and insanitary, and plagues often carried off their victims. The Anglo-Saxon Chronicle records many disasters and frequent fightings.

I have pointed out in my former book how these communities managed their affairs, the assemblies at their moot-hall, their Hundred Courts, and modes of administering justice, the formation of shires, and need not repeat what I have there recorded.[1] But there was one building which I have not yet mentioned, a very important one, and that is the village church. Of course, the English were wild pagans when they first invaded our shores, and plundered and destroyed all churches and monasteries erected by the British; but the time came when the Gospel message was brought to them by devoted missionaries, and they were converted to Christianity. The story of the conversion of England would take a long time to tell. Suffice it to say that by St. Augustine, St. Wilfrid, St. Birinus, and others in

[1] *English Villages*, pp. 86-89.

the south, and by the monks of Iona in the north, by St. Felix in the east, and other missionaries, the English became Christian; and in the time of Theodore, Archbishop of Canterbury, the thanes were encouraged to erect churches on their estates, and in most villages a plain wooden church arose with a house for the priest, who was supported by tithes contributed by the farmers and the lord.

Many monasteries, too, were founded by pious benefactors, and to these grants of lands and estates were made by kings and earls. The Chronicle of the Abbey of Abingdon records many such grants and charters. I give as an example the grant by King Edred to Athelwulf, of the village of Wittenham, in Berkshire:

"King Edred gave to Athelwulf, his earl, Wittenham, consisting of ten cassata (hides), and Athelwulf, with the consent of the King, granted the said villa by the same tenure by which the King had granted it to him, to God and the Blessed Virgin, and to this house of Abingdon and to the monks serving God in pure and perpetual charity."[1] Then follows the King's charter confirming the gift. Some of the motives of the donors are set forth in these charters, such as "for the forgiveness of his sins," "for the remedy of his soul," "in the expectation of obtaining a greater reward" and very strong curses and warnings are hurled at those who would dare to disregard the sanctity of the gifts or to deprive the monks of them.

A vast change was wrought in our villages. A

[1] *Historia Monasterii de Abingdon*, i., p. 134.

new influence was felt. Men turned from darkness to light. The clergy exercised a powerful influence over all classes, whether they were thanes and lords, or cottiers or slaves. They rescued the theows from slavery. In Ælfric's homilies they declared that "all Christian men are brothers, whether high or low, noble or ignoble, lord or slave. The wealthy are not better on that account than the needy. We are all alike before God, unless any one excel another in good works. As boldly may the slave call God his Father, as the King."[1] And when that good Archbishop died, his will directed that every Englishman who had lost his liberty during his episcopy should be freed. The clergy watched over the poor, the widow, and the orphan, and were not afraid to threaten with dire penalties any tyrannical oppressor or iniquitous lord. But it were vain to attempt to describe the vast change which the Church effected in village life in this volume.

The early preachers brought the Gospel message to the village, and often set up a cross of stone. Many of these remain, and some I have already described elsewhere[2]—wondrous examples of Saxon art. And soon a church was built. At first, as I have said, it would be constructed of timber, but soon a stone building would be erected. Often, in our existing churches, we find some walling or a doorway, and sometimes even a whole church that was reared by Saxon masons a thousand years ago. There is that precious little Saxon church at

[1] *Ælfric's Homilies*, i., p. 261.
[2] *English Villages*, pp. 95-101.

Bradford-on-Avon, that other one at Deerhurst in Gloucestershire. Architectural experts often discover in our ancient churches relics of pre-Conquest Saxon buildings that have been little suspected by our forefathers; and on the spots we worship God to-day in a building that has often been renewed, enlarged, restored, our English ancestors first learned to chant their psalms and hymns in praise of Jesus Christ our Saviour, to pray and worship Him.

Antiquaries delight in discovering relics of the past life of our ancient ancestors, and have found many traces of the Anglo-Saxon period in burial-mounds and graves and cemeteries. An examination of barrows shows the different customs of the various races. The Angles who settled in East Anglia practised cremation and urn burial, which was not so common amongst the Jutes who settled in Kent, Hampshire, and the Isle of Wight, or the Saxons of Essex, Sussex, and Wessex. The fibulæ or brooches found in the graves of these tribes differ considerably in shape and size. A large number of articles of personal adornment are found in these Saxon graves. A warrior's weapons were buried with him, a head and spike of his spear, heads of javelins, a long iron broad-sword, a long knife, occasionally an axe, and over his breast the iron boss of his shield is found, the wooden part having decayed away. In a mound in Taplow churchyard a fine set of weapons was found, and can be seen in the British Museum. A Saxon cemetery was discovered at Reading. Those who were interred there were Christians, and the body of a priest was discovered with a chalice buried with him. It is now in the Reading Museum. In pre-Christian times bodies were buried in a sitting or crouching position, as in a grave on Lady Wantage's estate, the contents of which I exhibited before the Society of Antiquaries. Fibulæ and buckles, made of bronze, and very beautifully ornamented, and gold fibulæ of circular form, have been found in the Kentish barrows, frequently ornamented with real or fictitious gems. Rings, bracclets, necklaces of beads, pendants for the neck and ears, are common. The beads are of glass, or amber, or variegated clay. Hairpins, châtelains with tweezers for removing superfluous hairs, tooth-picks, scissors, bone combs, small knives, glass drinking-vessels, bronze bowls, dishes and basins, have been found in Saxon graves, and occasionally buckets. A pair of dice was discovered in a grave at Kingston Down, perhaps a lucky pair that had brought the owner wealth, indicating a favourite pastime of the Saxons. There is much else to record concerning our Saxon forefathers, but we have a long road to traverse, and I must pass on to a new phase of our village life.

CHAPTER VII

THE VILLAGES AFTER THE NORMAN CONQUEST

Norman Conquest—Forest laws—Feudalism—Manor courts—Domesday Survey — Manor - house — Sutton Courtney — Norman hall—Chapel—Little Hempston—Lower Brockhampton—Plan of village.

THE effects of the Norman Conquest were not immediately felt by the villagers, at least by those remote from the actual scenes of fighting. An ingenious writer, the Hon. F. C. Baring, conceived the idea of tracing the course of William the Conqueror's march by the serious diminution of the value of the various villages that lay in his route. The inhabitants of those places suffered greatly; the Anglo-Saxon Chronicle states that he plundered all the country he overran; but life went on for a time much as usual in the countrysides remote from the scenes of battle and pillage, save that the men and women were greatly alarmed at beholding " such a token in the heavens as no man ever before saw. Some men said that was cometa, the star which some men call the haired star," portending terrible misfortunes. It was, doubtless, responsible for the defeat of the English at Senlac, or, as it is usually called, the Battle of Hastings. It certainly foretold misfortunes for the conquered.

At first, however, all went well; but then the

villagers saw their own lord dispossessed, and his land bestowed by the new King on some haughty Norman adventurer who had helped him to win the English crown, and who treated them like slaves, and called them "English swine." He deprived all the English earls and thanes and bishops of their estates, save those "who bowed the knee to Baal," swore allegiance to him, and accepted his rule. Such a one was Earl Bigod, lord of Wallingford, whose daughter was married to one of William's chieftains, Robert D'Oyley. Some of William's followers received vast estates, sometimes as many as 139 manors, while others had to content themselves with some small manor. A complete system of feudalism was established. The term "manor" came in with the Normans, but it was only the old Saxon village with a new name. The same system of agriculture continued, and the same country life went on. The expulsion of the Saxon landed gentry indeed created a vast disturbance in the minds of their tenants and servants, and they loathed their new lord with a wild hatred; but the Conqueror was a cunning king, and did not wish to disturb the farmers and cottiers. He wanted the people to be content with their new masters. He required soldiers for his army, and ordered the manor lords to provide men-at-arms, and to perform their duties to him as their supreme sovereign. "Feudalism grasps all England in its iron fingers, and the pitiless accuracy of Domesday Book leaves no loophole of escape."[1]

[1] *History of English Landed Interest*, by R. M. Garnier, i. 123.

What became of the dispossessed thanes? Some of them took to the woods and became outlaws, like Hereward the Wake, or fled abroad to the Low Countries, and carved out their fortunes with their good broadswords. And it was woe to the English peasants when the Norman lord came to live amongst them. He was very different from their old Saxon squire. He despised them, was haughty and contemptuous. He had no respect for their old customs. He levied heavy taxes upon them, and required additional services and tributes in food or money. He showed them no mercy. The socmen and geburs who had enjoyed much freedom under the rule of their Saxon lord were degraded and lost their rights and privileges. The new lord seized more land for his own use, and the King did likewise when he needed it to satisfy his passion for the chase. Both he and his Norman adventurers loved hunting, and there is that terrible story of his afforesting three thousand acres in Hampshire, destroying manors and cornlands, and towns and villages, and hamlets and churches, in order to find homes for "the tall stag which he loved as though he were their father," and undisturbed lair for the wild boars. Even the power of the Church he defied. The monks of Abingdon claimed to have sporting rights in Windsor Forest in the parish of Winkfield, granted to them by the pious King Edward the Confessor. Our Berkshire lands were famous for hunting, and the King did not see why these monks should deprive him of his pleasure. The monks and the people protested against this royal usurpation. They went in a body to Windsor Castle, but they were obliged to own defeat, as the governor there was too many for them, and too strong to be resisted or intimidated.

As the King did, so did his lords. Forest laws, merciless and cruel, were enacted, inflicting fearful penalties of death or mutilation on man or dog if caught in chasing the deer. Trespass upon the royal hunting grounds, or the slaughter of a wild beast, was punished with the same severity and penalty that was inflicted upon the robber or the murderer. The culprit was doomed to death or mutilation, the loss of an eye or a hand. Dogs were expeditated—*i.e.*, the balls of their feet were cut out—so as to prevent them from hunting. But, in spite of the numerous forest officials, wardens, verderers, foresters, agisters, regarders, keepers, bailiffs, and beadles, there were many outlaws in the forests, such as Adam de Gurdon, who haunted Windsor Forest and defied capture; and there is the romantic story of Fulke Fitz-Warren who was outlawed in John's reign, having in his youth incurred the Prince's resentment by winning from him a game at chess.

With the Normans came the full development of the manor on feudal lines. As we have seen, the old Saxon "tun" or village corresponded fairly exactly with the Continental manor, but there existed institutions that were unknown across the Channel. There was the village folkmoot for settling the affairs of the community; and each village sent its representatives to the Hundred Court, and above the Hundred was the Shire Moot. The Conqueror was wise enough to retain these popular arrangements, but he established in each manor a Court Baron or Manorial Court for administering justice and settling the domestic affairs of the manor. This was intended to supersede the folkmoot, but the latter in many cases contrived to survive. There was also a Court Leet in each manor for trying criminal offences and breaches of the law of the realm.

And here it may be advisable to open that priceless book, the Domesday Survey, which William ordered to be compiled mainly for the purpose of discovering the amount of taxation that was due to the royal exchequer. It was a Geld book, a tax or rate book, intended to furnish the royal officers with sufficient information to enable them to decide what changes were necessary, in order that all England might be taxed in accordance with a just and uniform plan. Although from Abbey Chronicles and Charters some earlier information may be gathered about some villages, the Domesday Book is practically the starting-point of all local history. The Conqueror was at Gloucester in the winter of 1085, and had deep speech with his wise men The compilation of this wonderful book was devised, and legates or justices were ordered to collect all the information that was desired. The following were the chief points: (1) The owner of the manor; (2) the name of the former owner in the time of King Edward the Confessor; (3) the number of hides or carucates, or ploughlands;[1] (4) the number

[1] A ploughland was the amount of land annually ploughable by one team of oxen.

of plough oxen; (5) of villeins; (6) of cottiers or *bordarii;* (7) of slaves; (8) the extent of the surrounding woodland, as estimated by the hogs for which it would provide pasturage. Sometimes a church and its priests are mentioned, if the church-land paid taxes; also the mill wherein all the tenants were obliged to bring their corn to be ground. The increase or decrease, as compared with the time of the Confessor, was noted, and sometimes the animals on the farm, the *runci* or baggage horses, the wild mares (*equæ sylvaticæ*); but cows, sheep, and goats are seldom mentioned, as not being employed in agriculture. Sheep, as well as cows and goats, supplied the people with milk.

For the historian all this information is, of course, most valuable, and as an example of these parochial records I will give the facsimile of the Domesday entry of the little village of Barkham, where it is my lot to live:

IN CERLEDONE H̅D̅.

Rex teñ in dñio Berchehã. Ælmer tenuit de rege E. Tc̃ 7 m̊ p iii hid. Tr̃ a ẽ iii cãr. In dñio c̃ una 7 vi uilli 7 iiii borđ cũ iii cãr. Ibi v ãc pti. Silua de XL porc. Valuit iiii lib T.R.E. 7 m̊: iii lib.

TRANSLATION.

In the Hundred of Charlton.

The King holds Barkham in demesne. Ælmer held it of King Edward (the Confessor). Then, as now, it was rated for three hides. The land is three ploughlands. In demesne there is one ploughland. There are six villeins, four borderers with three ploughs. There are five acres of pasture. Wood for the pasturage of forty hogs. It was worth £4 in the time of King Edward, afterwards, and now £3.

This is not so large or so elaborate a description of a manor as we find in connection with more important places than Barkham, but it will serve to illustrate the Domesday Survey of a village, and the minuteness of the details set forth therein.

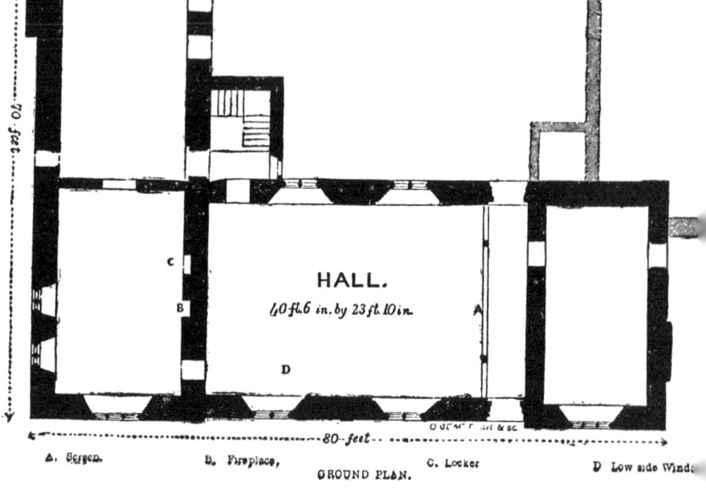

PLAN OF SUTTON COURTNEY, BERKSHIRE
(From Hone's *Manor and Manorial Records*)

The manor is "an estate or district in which the central house is the hall." Such is the definition given us by Professor Vinogradoff. It will be advisable, therefore, to look first at this central building and its occupant. A few Norman houses are still in existence. At Sutton Courtney, in Berkshire, there is a building which was part of the Norman manor-hall, and was the chapel of the house. The rest of this early dwelling-place has vanished. Its date is about A.D. 1200. The arches of the two doorways are round, but the dog-tooth ornament and the lancet windows disclose its Early English character. The same village is rich in manor-houses. A very charming Elizabethan house took the place of the Norman hall just mentioned, and opposite to it, across the road, is the old manor-house of the monks of Abingdon, of which an illustration is given. The hall (40 feet by 24 feet) is nearly perfect, and its old oaken roof remains, very lofty, supported by king-posts with struts resting on wooden arches which rise from stone corbels carved into heads. The windows have been altered; formerly they were lofty, with pointed heads carried up through the roof in a number of dormers. Under one of the windows is a remarkable low-side window with good decorated tracery, and the hooks for hanging its shutter still remain. On the north of the hall is a passsage called the screens. The house has two wings. The solar is lighted by two decorated windows. This manor-house was built by the monks in the middle of the fourteenth century. The Norman hall differed not in plan from its Saxon predecessor, but it was a much finer building. The manor-house of Appleton, Berkshire, a twelfth-century structure, is of a simple oblong plan, and has round-headed arches with Early English mouldings. Boothby Pagnell manor-house, in Lincolnshire, is a good example of a twelfth-century building. It consists of a large hall with windows high up in the wall, one of which is a later addition. It is a plain oblong house divided into a large and a small chamber. The hall is on the first floor, reached by steps, with a vaulted undercroft beneath. Warneford, in Hampshire, has the simplest form of the hall and offices. Two rows of tall pillars

(From Baring-Gould's *Old Country Life*)

carried the principal timbers of the roof, and a passage separated the hall from the offices. Together with barns and other out-buildings the manor-house was in the form of a quadrangle. By degrees, as time went on, there was a greater desire for comfort and the privacy of the family life. Hence, additional rooms were added. There was the "solar," usually built towards the south, so that the sunshine might stream in, and warm and light the apartment. It served as the private chamber of the lord and his family; and above it were often situated the sleeping-rooms, divided by rude partitions, which were reached by a stone staircase that was sometimes exterior to the building, so that you would have to go outside into the wind and rain in order to reach your bedroom. The buttery, or storeroom for provisions, wine, and ale, was on the side of the hall remote from the dais end, and above it was the bower, or the women's chamber.

A prominent feature of the manor-house was the chapel. In some cases, as at Little Wenham, this consisted of an oratory separated from the hall by a screen; in some other houses it was a separate building. I have seen at East Hendred and other places a curious arrangement. At the west end the chapel had two floors, but at the east end the upper floor terminated some six feet or more from the east wall, where the altar stood and where the chaplain officiated. Hence he had two congregations, one in the upper story, and the other below. In the upper space the lord of the manor and his family worshipped, and in the lower the servants made their devotions. The late Mr. Hone discovered in the Liberate Rolls of Henry III. an order by the King for a chapel to be constructed at his house at Kennington "in such a manner that, in the upper part, there may be a chapel for the use of our Queen, so that she may enter that chapel from her chamber, and in the lower part let there be a chapel for the use of the household." It needed little alteration from this arrangement for window-openings to look down into the chapel from the bedchambers as at Broughton Castle, upon observing which the witty Bishop Wilberforce remarked that he never understood before so clearly the meaning of the verse in the Psalms: "Let the saints rejoice in their beds."

We like to picture the life of the inhabitants of these primitive manor-houses, the lady sitting with her maids working their tapestry with figures of swans and beasts and ships and heroes, the playing of games in the courtyard, the men returning from their hunting, feasting in the hall, the minstrels and jugglers contributing to their amusement, the former chanting the Song of Roland and other stirring lays of romance and war.

Although we are now in Norman times, it may be well here to trace the development of the manor-house during the mediæval period, in order that we need not be obliged to recur to the subject again. In my book on *The Manor Houses of England* I have given many other examples of Norman dwellings. These were all of simple plan such as I have already described, and even the royal palaces at Clarendon, Kennington, Woodstock, and others contained no additional accommodation. Even in the thirteenth century few alterations were made. In my former book I gave as an example of this period the interesting house at Charney Basset in Berkshire, which has as its chief feature the hall; and the chambers at each side are arranged as wings, so as to form with the hall three sides of a quadrangle or courtyard. A chapel or oratory adjoins the solar in the south wing.

A perfect example of a fourteenth-century manor-house is that of Little Hempston, near Totnes, which

(From Baring-Gould's *Old Country Life*)

is practically unaltered since that period. Mr. Baring-Gould thus describes it:

It consists of a quadrangle with buildings on all four sides; but the central court is only 20 feet by 12 feet, into which all the windows look from sunless rooms. The only exception is the hall window, which has a southern outlook. The hall was heated by a brazier in the centre, and the smoke went out at a louvre in the roof. There was one gloomy parlour with a fireplace in it opening out of the hall. The rest of the quadrangle was taken up with

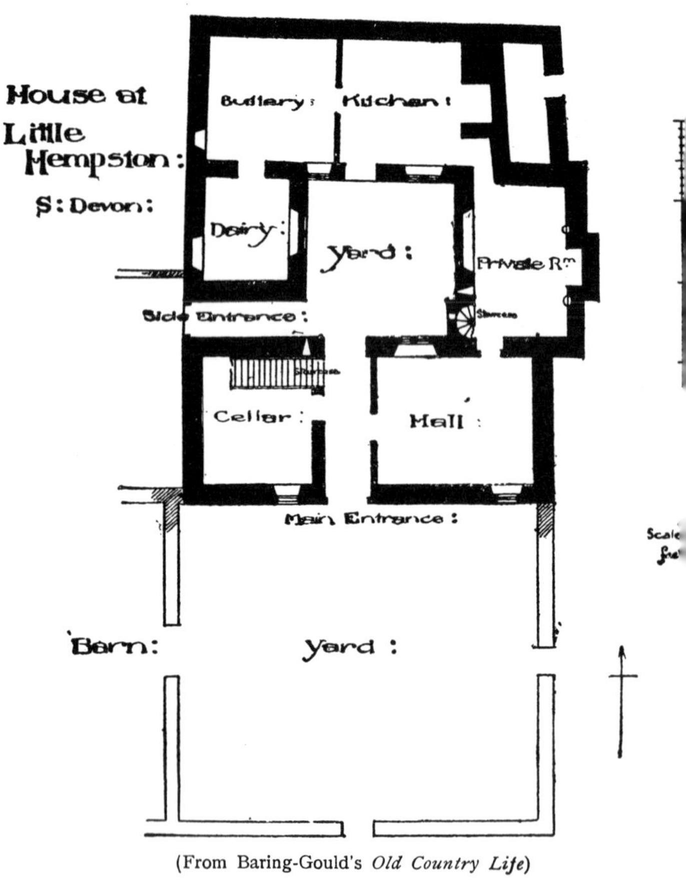

(From Baring-Gould's *Old Country Life*)

kitchen, porter's lodge, cellar, and stable. Upstairs one long dormitory ![1]

[1] *Old Country Life*, by S. Baring-Gould.

Lower Brockhampton Hall is of the same date, and has a hall with a noble roof and minstrels' gallery, and also a detached gatehouse. These houses were usually guarded by a surrounding moat. The manor-house of Great Chalfield is a typical example of a fifteenth-century structure. It still exists in all its beauty, and has been in recent years renovated and conservatively restored. A moat surrounds it. You enter the forecourt through a gateway on the west. On the east side of the courtyard stands a beautiful chapel, and on the south stands the fine old little mansion. There is a great hall with solar on the east side. The screens, or passage, are on the west with buttery, pantry, kitchen, etc. A range of buildings occupies the west of the court, and barns and stables stand outside it nigh the entrance gate. The Norman manor-house looked out upon the village, with its clustering tenants and its curious system of agriculture, which I have tried already to describe. The Conquest made little difference to the work of the tenants and labourers in the fields. Still, each villein had his scattered strips of arable land, his homestead with closes for the pasturage of his cattle, and his share of the pasturage in the common fields when the crops had been gathered. The accompanying plan gives a fair notion of the appearance of the village. The lord of the manor with two of his huntsmen are riding away to chase the deer or the wild boar in the forest. In the centre is his demesne land with the manor-house and church. The houses of the tenants line the

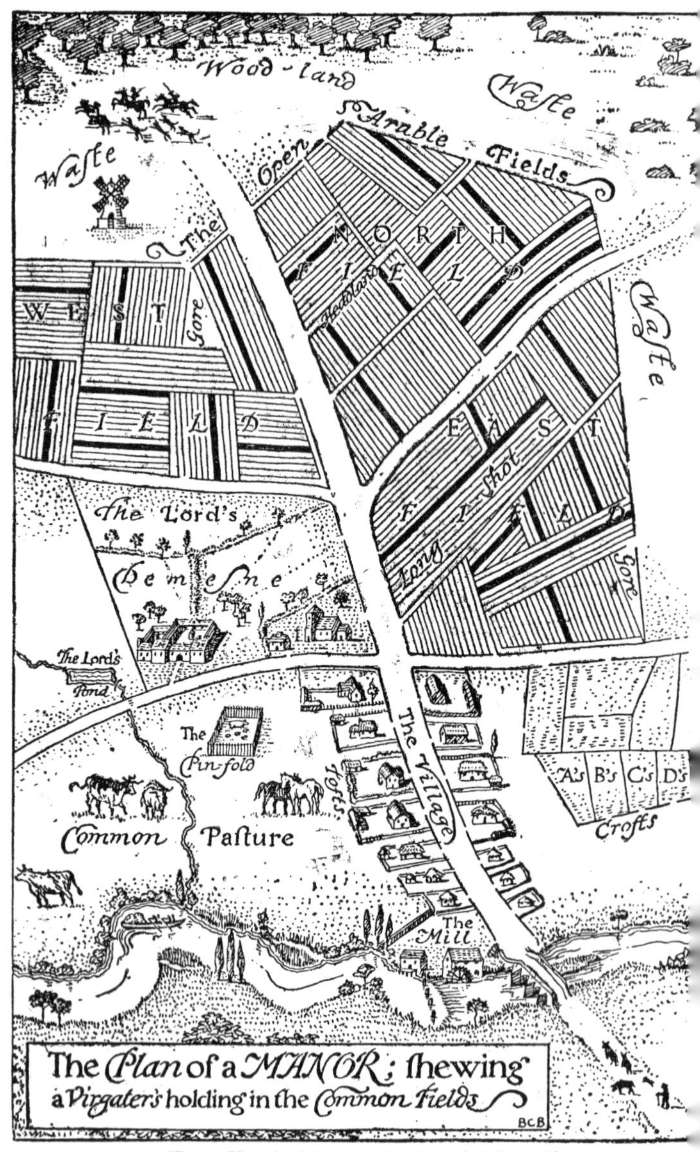

(From Hone's *Manor and Manorial Records*)

village street, on the left of which is the common pasture with lowing kine and horses grazing, and in the centre stands the pinfold. A brook runs through the lord's fish-pond which provided him with some savoury meals, and on the river bank stands his mill, to which all the tenants were bound to bring their corn to be ground. On the right are the special closes of richer meadow land for some of the principal farmers. The long parallel lines represent the arable fields divided into acre or half-acre strips.

In my account of the Saxon village I have tried to explain the methods of farming, which continued during the Norman period and for centuries later. We get our land measures from this system. The furlong, or "furrow long," was the longest furrow that a team of oxen could plough without stopping to rest—*i.e.*, about two hundred and twenty yards. The ploughman used an ox-goad to urge on his oxen. This goad was a rod with a very persuasive iron point at the end for pricking the beasts. In order to reach his oxen this rod was about sixteen and a half feet in length—*i.e.*, the length of a rod, pole, or perch. Mr. Hone points out that the ploughman's ox-goad would naturally be used as a land measure, and that the ploughman would place it at right angles to his first furrow in order to see how much land he had to till. Four of these lands or roods make up the acre, the day's work of the ploughman, who would then drive his beasts home well satisfied with his labour:

> Something attempted, something done
> Had earned a night's repose.

But all the land would not lend itself to this symmetrical arrangement. Odd corners would be left in the fields, and these were termed gores or gored acres; and sometimes bits of land were hardly worth the trouble of being ploughed, and these were left uncultivated and called no man's land.

Nothing is so changeless as agriculture. The same order goes on year after year. Son succeeds father and cultivates the same lands his sire tilled, observing the same rules of rotation of crops. Occasionally there are a few breaks and revolutions in farming. We shall note some in the fourteenth and in the sixteenth century, when the rich English fleeces brought much gain, and ploughing was neglected and the labourers fled to the towns, and cottages were pulled down; but ere the century closed they all came back again, and the old methods went on until the eighteenth century brought into being the Enclosure Acts which revolutionised everything, and the old common-field system, a very wasteful form of agriculture, vanished, and new times and new manners dawned with varying fortunes for farmers and labourers. But all this belongs to a later period of village life, and not to the time when the Norman lord ruled over our English forefathers, who sometimes groaned beneath his tyrannical sway.

CHAPTER VIII

THE VILLAGE CHURCH

The village church—Its plan—Norman architecture—Subsequent alterations—Gothic art—Church furniture—Archbishop Packham's instructions—Mediæval parish life—Power of the Church.

THERE is one building in the village to which attention must now be drawn, and that is the village church which, as our plan shows, nestles near the manor-house, and is the great centre of the life of the village. It is not usually noticed in the Domesday Survey, as that document concerned itself mainly with fiscal matters, and with the amount of taxation that was due to the Royal Exchequer, and however much his unfortunate successor has to pay in rates and taxes the rector of Norman times was usually free from such heavy burdens. The church was there, though Domesday does not always mention it. We have already mentioned the Saxon structure, remains of which are often found incorporated in the later building, but with the coming of the Normans there was a considerable development of architectural skill and energy. Peace seemed to have fallen on this distracted island. No longer did hordes of Danes sweep through the land, destroying wherever they went. Stone churches replaced the thatched wooden shrines with which many of the Saxon villagers had hitherto been content; although there were many stone churches prior to the Norman Conquest, and the Danes, when they became civilised and Christianised, had rebuilt in stone the churches which they had destroyed. Under Canute the Church had flourished; he encouraged the building of churches, and an era of church building had been inaugurated. Dr. Freeman tersely states: "The nation was intensely religious, and the Church was intensely national." During the reign of Edward the Confessor there was much progress in architectural skill; but the advent of William caused a vast increase in the number of churches in England. Within seventy years from the accession of Canute to the compilation of the Domesday Survey, no less than one thousand seven hundred churches were built, and the good work increased rapidly until most villages had their church, sometimes erected by the lord of the manor, but everywhere recognised as the spiritual home of the people, who often contributed to the cost of the building or gave freely their labour for the erection of God's House.

The ordinary plan of the churches erected during this Norman period was that of a cross with a low tower rising at the intersection of the nave and choir with the transepts. The choir was usually short, with frequently an apsidal termination at the east end. The eastern sides of the transepts often had chapels or chantries. The walls were thick, and therefore did not require strong buttresses, only projecting very slightly from their surface; they appear to have been placed there more for ornament than for use, for breaking the surface of the walls rather than to add to their strength. The doorways are remarkable for their sculpture, and the masons seem to have exhausted their skill and ingenuity in devising curiously carved tympana—that is to say, the space above the portal and below the arch. We find such subjects represented as Our Lord in Majesty, the Agnus Dei, Adam and Eve, St. George and the Dragon, the Tree of Life, the Signs of the Zodiac, St. Michael fighting Satan, and many others. The masons of the period had a very exuberant fancy, and nothing came amiss to them. They loved to expatiate in the religious mysticism of the age, and to embody in speaking stone the favourite legends of local saints. They exercised their art, not only on the tympana, but also in the carving of fonts and in mural paintings. Men, animals, fishes, birds, plants, agricultural operations, hunting and hawking; the saint, the bishop, the priest, the warrior; heraldic and conventional forms of creatures, living and dead, were worked up with surprising ingenuity and ever-varying forms of delineation. Their work forms a very fascinating study, but it is beyond our purpose to pursue it here.

As we look at our Norman church we notice a great variety of mouldings, small and narrow windows, massive piers and arches, cushion capitals frequently ornamented with the scallop or volute which they copied from the work of the Romans, who themselves imitated the Greek sculptors.

Every one knows that the Norman arch is semicircular headed, which, during the later and Transition period, gave place to the pointed. The Norman masons were fond of decorating their walls with arcading, and also inserted sculptured corbels and gargoyles, those curious grotesque heads, through which water was carried off from the roofs.

Such, in brief, was the village church as it originally stood. It has been much altered in subsequent times. Aisles have been added later, larger windows inserted in the Decorated or Perpendicular period. In the thirteenth century the masons were striving after constructive lightness and elegance. They wanted to build larger and finer buildings, and to abandon the old massive pillars, heavy arches, and curious and unnatural decorations. All through the Gothic period of art we see that they were always "striving after a more excellent way." They manifested the hunger of the heart after the unattainable, that is ever seeking but never finding actual perfection, and yet never stays in its seeking or abandons effort.

The growth of Gothic art in this country was entirely an English development. It owed little or nothing to foreign influence. It was not imported by masons brought over from France, but was conceived, developed, and perfected by our own people. It was no exotic art, no alien welcomed to our shores, but a true English native art born in the brains and faith of our English forefathers, and nourished here with a nation's wholehearted affection. Iconoclastic "Goths and Vandals" of ancient and modern times have done their best to mutilate or destroy our churches, sometimes to remove them altogether, and erect in their places fearful examples of Victorian Gothic or weird fancies of their own. But a very large number remain that have happily escaped, and exist to this day very much in the condition that their builders left them. Therefore, we should be grateful to these men who did their best to make the church, their spiritual house, the great house of the parish, as fair and beautiful as they knew how. It was not the great men, the nobles and princes, who did the work. It was the men of the village who put their heart into their work, and wrought in homely style sweet, natural, and unaffected as William Morris wrote, "an art of peasants, rather than of merchant princes or courtiers; and it must be a hard heart that does not love it, whether a man has been born among it like ourselves, or has come wonderingly on its simplicity from all the grandeur over seas."

Not only the fabric, but the furniture was worthy of the high dignity of this village House of God. It was no mean dwelling of the Most High. Even small village churches possessed a great wealth of furniture, and of the accessories of Divine worship. A Venetian traveller in this country in 1500 observed: "There is not a parish church in the kingdom so mean as not to possess crucifixes, candlesticks, censers, patens, and cups of silver." The report of the Commissioners of King Edward VI. containing the inventories of furniture and ornaments of parish churches in several counties abundantly supports the observation of the Venetian. These inventories enable us to form some notion of the beauty and costliness of the ornaments with which even our smaller parish churches by the devotion and piety of the parishioners had been endowed. I will give only one example, that of the village church of Aldermaston, in Berkshire. The Commissioners reported as follows:

iij belles weyinge xvi^c A saunse bell[1] weyinge halfe a hunderd A hande bell weyinge v pounde ij Candlestickes of brase weyinge LX^li ij Smale Candilstickes weyinge vi^li ij Crosses of lattene[2] weynge ij^li one cross of led weynge A pounde and A halfe A peyre of Cruettes[3] of Tyne[4] price iiij A halywater pott of brasse weynge ij^li a Certene of owlde geron[5] weying xii^li A cope of Russett[6] veluytt iij vestmonts on Sattene Bridges[7] bordered w^t gold one of whyte damaske[8] and one of black fustane apes[9] ij Surplices iij Towelles one of dyaper and ij of lynene ij corprisses of veluyt ibrotherd w^t golde[10] A Chalyse of Sylver percell gylt weynge xviij ownces. A pixe of lattene weynge half A li[11] a canopy[12] w^t A couveringe of ffustiane apes A banner Clothe of Sylke & ij owld Stremers ij Cruettes price iiij A Sacrynge bell[13] price ij^d pyllowbers[14] price viij^d v owld Alter Clothes.

[1] Sanctus bell.

[2] Of latten metal, or a fine kind of brass.

[3] The flasks, or cruets, containing wine and water used at the altar. When in pairs, the letter V (*vinum*) was engraved on one, and A (*aqua*) on the other.

[4] Tin.

[5] Iron.

[6] Of russet or brown colour.

[7] Satin from Bruges.

[8] Cloth of Damascus.

[9] Fustian from Naples.

[10] Each corporal was of velvet embroidered with gold.

[11] Half a pound.

[12] A hood or tabernacle over the altar under the shadow of which the pix was suspended.

[13] Sacring or sacrament bell that was rung by the server at Mass at the most sacred and solemn parts of the service.

[14] Cushions on the altar for the altar-book.

Ex uno disce omnes. Such was the list of valuables in one little church, and there were others that may be mentioned. Perhaps I ought to explain that a pix is a box or vessel in which the consecrated bread in Holy Communion is reverently preserved for the purpose of giving communion to the sick and infirm, who are unable to attend the service in church. A good example is preserved in the Ashmolean Museum at Oxford. The "corprisse," or corporal, is a square piece of linen or other material, so called because the *corpus* or Sacramental Body of Christ is placed on it during the Mass. At Aldermaston there was a cope, one of the most magnificent of clerical vestments; we find them to have been in general use in many other village churches. Thus, there were two at Avington, another little Berkshire church. A cope is a vestment cut in an exact semicircle like a cloak, attached to which is a hood, formerly used as such, but now merely an ornamental appendage covered with decoration. Along the straight edge of the semicircle runs the orphrey, a band of embroidery usually representing the figures of saints, heraldic or symbolical devices, and adorned with jewels, pearls, or precious metals. At another small church there were three copes, one of black damask, another of bright green satin embroidered with gold wire, and a third of red silk and green wrought together. Our reformers seem to have retained its use at least in cathedrals and larger churches, though our village churches were pillaged of them.

The parishes were ordered by law to provide all

things necessary for the services. In 1280 Archbishop Peckham directed that they should find such goods as vestments, chalice, missal, processional cross, paschal candles, etc.; and twenty-five years later Archbishop Winchelsey increased the list of parochial duties, requiring the people to find the following:

Legend,[1] Antiphonal,[2] Grayle,[3] Psalter, Tropary,[4] Ordinale, Missal,[5] Manual,[6] Chalice, the best Vestment with Chasuble,[7] Dalmatic[8] and Tunicle,[9] and a Cope for the choir with all their belongings (that is, amice,[10] girdle, maniple[11] and stole, etc.), the frontal for the High Altar, with three cloths; three surplices, a rochet,[12] the processional cross, a cross to carry to the sick, a thurible,[13] a lantern, a bell to ring when the Body of Christ is carried to the sick; a pyx of ivory or silver for the Body of Christ, the Lenten veil;[14] the Rogation Day banner;[15] the bells with

[1] A book of lessons from Holy Scripture.

[2] A service-book containing all the offices and the Mass, used by the cantors at the antiphon-lectern which stood in the centre of the choir.

[3] Grayle, or gradual, a book containing all the musical portions of the Mass.

[4] Tropary or troparium, a volume containing the tropes or sequences, being verses sung before the Gospel in the Mass.

[5] The Book of the Mass. [6] A small portable service-book.

[7] Eucharistic vestment. [8] A long robe with sleeves.

[9] A robe similar to the dalmatic but plainer and shorter.

[10] An ornamented linen collar worn over the surplice.

[11] Originally a strip of fine linen worn over the left wrist of the celebrant to wipe the chalice; subsequently an ornament.

[12] A frock of white lawn with tight sleeves worn by the higher dignitaries in the church.

[13] A vessel of metal for incense.

[14] During Lent a veil was hung before the high altar. In a Berkshire church the pulley by which it was raised or lowered remains.

[15] During Rogation-tide or " Gang Week " the bounds of the parish were beaten. Reference will be made to this custom later on.

their cords; a bier to carry the dead upon; the Holy Water vat;[1] the osculatorium for the Pax;[2] the Paschal candlestick;[3] a font with its lock and key; the images in the church; the image of the patron Saint in the chancel; the enclosure wall of the cemetery; and all repairs of every sort, except those of the chancel which pertain to the Rectors or Vicars.

One would imagine that the people and the churchwardens would groan over these very numerous requirements of their ecclesiastical superiors; but they do not seem to have done so. The various churchwardens' accounts and the church inventories abundantly show that the people were always eager to maintain and beautify their churches, and considered no money or labour too great a charge for improving God's House. Sometimes there was a little wholesome rivalry between two neighbouring parishes, and if one village church had six bells, its neighbour would not rest satisfied until a like number sent forth a gladsome peal from its ivy-clad tower.

Cardinal Gasquet in his *Mediæval Parish Life* records the personal efforts of the parishioners to improve their church. Some rich man gives a costly silver-gilt monstrance, another three copes of purple velvet, while "old Moder Hopper" presents two long candlesticks and a towel on the

[1] On special festivals the clerk used to visit the principal parishioners carrying this vat, which contained holy water, and with the *aspergillum* sprinkling them. This was also done in church.

[2] An ornament by which the kiss of peace was given to the faithful. In England it was termed the "pax-brede."

[3] For holding the Paschal candle that was lighted at services during the Easter season.

rood of our Lady's chancel. When a steeple was decided upon, the owner of a quarry gave the stone, and the churchwardens and people bought a tree and engaged a carpenter, and cut up the tree and made boards for the scaffolding, and for the spire itself; and they bought lime for the mortar and tubs to make it in, and everyone lent a hand when the day's work was over, and toiled early and late to raise their steeple. Every year they tried to add something to their store of treasures, a new sanctus bell, or a pair of censer chains, or a new lectern, or a new vestment. Thus it seems to have been everywhere. The church was very dear to the hearts of the people. The Cardinal calls special attention to the little hamlet of Morebath, a small, remote parish on the borders of Exmoor, where none but poor people dwelt, and earned their bread by hard and incessant toil. And yet there were no less than eight Guilds or Societies, or Fraternities who maintained altars in the church. In 1538 they made a voluntary rate to buy a new cope, and collected £3 6*s.* 8*d.* Four years before this the chalice was stolen; so the young men and maidens took the matter up, and bought a new chalice without any charge on the parish. On another occasion, when they wanted a new cope, a woman gave her "gown and a ring," and another "a cloak and girdle," and a good man contributed "seven sheep and 3*s.* 4*d.* in money."

There were many objects in the church on which they expended their money and their pains. There was the rood-screen, finely carved and often em-

THE SACRAMENT OF BAPTISM
(from *The Art of Good Lyvinge*)

bellished with paintings of the Apostles or other Saints, and above it stood the rood. The walls were covered with mural paintings and colour brightened the stone carvings and the tombs. A niche for a lamp, new choir books, sedilia and piscina, hangings at the back and side of the altars, stained glass for the windows, were all objects of reverent regard; and numerous wills are in existence which show how this or that benefactor left money for the care and beautifying of the church he loved.

In addition to their regard for the sacred building as a symbol of their religion and the expression of their reverential homage to the Most High, the parishioners owed much to their church. It had a temporal, as well as a spiritual, power. The rector could defy the power of the most tyrannical of manor-lords. He had behind him a good bishop who was as strong or stronger than the lord, and in the distance in the City of the Seven Hills there sat one, who, though his decrees were often disregarded and disputed by independent and freedom-loving Englishmen, nevertheless could bring some powerful influences to bear upon those who dared to injure the Church. But there was still a greater power that prevented any injustice being done to the parson and his flock. When the lord attended the services he saw over the chancel arch a very realistic painting of a Doom. There was St. Michael weighing souls, and the good being conducted by angels to the abodes of happiness and bliss, and there was a huge Satan with terrified victims being dragged by demons to the fearful horrors of a very realistic hell, where devils are torturing the miserable creatures who in life had offended against the Divine laws. There is a usurer having his eyes poked out, a dishonest tradesman, a cheating milkman, and a roguish smith reposing on a bridge of spikes, and sundry other sinners suffering agonies for their crimes. However much the powerful lord might dare to defy the parson and the bishop, and even say scornful things about the Pope, he would remember his latter end, and deal fairly and justly in matters of religion; and of this the village folk were not unmindful.

CHAPTER IX

MANORIAL TENANTS

Classes of tenants of the manor—Freemen or yeomen—Saxon customs of gavelkind and borough-English survived—Villeins — Bordarii — Tradesmen — Norman names — Adulterine castles.

IN the map of a manor we saw the houses of the tenants lining the village street. These were of various classes, and Domesday tells us their names, and the parts they played in the village community. They were, for the most part, customary tenants—that is to say, they held some land under the lord of the manor—and were bound to render some services in return for their holding, providing an ox or more for the plough team, and working for their lord on his own land or demesne two or more days in the week. At the head of the rural society were the freemen or sokemen, who as time went constantly increased their numbers. They paid a fixed sum as rent for their land, either in money or goods, or labour. They were not bound to the land like the villeins, and could leave their homes when they pleased. Some of them belonged to the families who had held their lands as their own property from time immemorial. As time went on these socmen or yeomen became numerous, and formed an important element in the life of the country. "The yeomen, the bowmen, the lads of dale and fell," made the best of warriors. By their prowess in the field, as followers of the lord, these men earned his gratitude and his friendship, and were rewarded with a grant of land, for which they rendered some service, such as I have already described in a previous chapter. Then many of the villein class improved their position, saved sufficient money to redeem them from compulsory service, and became freemen; and as in modern times people preferred the country to town life, and bought or reclaimed land in the woodlands around the village. All these freemen constituted an important element in the manorial system. Mr. Hone states:

> The tenure by which the freeholder held his land came in time to be distinguished by legal writers as tenure in free socage, and to denote an estate held by any certain and determinate service, as by fealty and a money rent, or by homage and fealty without rent.

He points out also that the continuation of the relics of Saxon liberty seems to show that many of these freemen were the actual descendants of the men who were landowners before the Conqueror came to England. The old Saxon customs of gavelkind and borough-English survived the Norman Conquest. Under the former the estate of a father was shared equally by all his sons; under the latter ultimogeniture prevailed—*i.e.*, the property passed to the youngest son. This custom prevails to the present day in Sussex and some other southern counties. This survival of Saxon law apparently indicates that its observers could proudly answer to the boastful Norman gentry

Sowing

Reaping

Threshing

Sheep Shearing

The Villein at Work
Hare ms., 1892

who said, "My ancestors came over with the Conqueror," "Yes, but we were here when the Conqueror came."

I must here describe the other dwellers in our ancestral village. By far the most numerous class were the villeins (*villani*) who corresponded to the Saxon *ceorls*. Each held about thirty acres in scattered acre or half-acre strips, a furlong in length and a rod or two in breadth, separated by turf balks. The villein thus supported himself and his family, and in return was bound to render certain services to his lord, to work on the home-farm, and to provide two or more oxen for the manorial plough-team. His work was of two kinds—week-work and boon-work. The former consisted of two or three days' labour a week, while the latter was performed during harvest or at other times of special agricultural pressure; and in addition to this he was required to pay a modest rent for his holding.

The villein was a very hard-worked individual, and his lack of freedom must have been galling, though he had his rights and legal protection from tyranny and oppression. However, he could not bring a legal action against his lord in the King's Courts, but he might obtain justice in the Court of his manor for wrongs or injuries, for trespasses and recover debts. He had to pay a fine, called merchet, when his daughter was married, but the *jus primo nocte* is an absurd legal fiction that was never recognised nor practised—at least in England. But he could not leave the village and go to work elsewhere. If he were an adventurous soul, sometimes he would steal away at night and fly to the nearest town, and there take up his abode and become a citizen; and such was the power of the boroughs of England that then no manor-lord could reclaim him. However, by paying a small fine to his lord, called clevage, he could live outside the borders of the manor. He required a licence if he went to the University or took Holy Orders. When he died his heirs received his lands and goods, but the lord could claim a heriot—that is, the best beast, whether ox or horse, or some other chattel. But his lot was not an unhappy one, as he possessed a good farm, and as time went on the condition of the villein was greatly improved, and all traces of servile bondage vanished. There was also a second class of villein, the semi-villein, whose holding was fifteen acres.

Lower in the social scale were the *bordarii*, or cottars (corresponding to our cottagers), who held only five acres. They kept no oxen, and therefore escaped the duty of ploughing the lord's land; but they usually worked for him one day in each week, hired their labour to the freemen, and corresponded to our agricultural labourers. Sometimes they were obliged during harvest to work on the demesne land, and to provide for the lord's table some eggs, or poultry, or honey. Some of the lowest class of cottars had only a quarter of an acre; and then there were the slaves. These were only few in number, we are pleased to discover, and in the next century, after the Conquest, they, as a class, entirely disappeared and were absorbed among the cottars.

Such were the dwellers in the village in the twelfth and thirteenth centuries. Moreover, each village was self-contained and supplied its own needs. No tradesmen's carts, as in modern times, came from the nearest town to provide them with necessaries, nor did they send for builders and carpenters from the town to repair their habitations. Every trade had its representative in the village. There was the *prepositus*, bailiff or reeve, who had many duties to perform, to which I shall refer again presently. He was assisted by a *bedellus*, beadle or under-bailiff. *Bovarii*, or ox-herds, looked after the plough-teams. The *carpentarius*, or carpenter; the *cementarius*, or bricklayer; the *custos apium*, or bee-keeper; the *faber*, or smith; the *molinarius*, or miller—were all important officers in the village, and in return for their services to the community had their lands in the common fields. There were also the *piscatores* (fishermen), *pistores* (bakers), *porcarii* (swine-herds), *viccarii* (cowmen), who were all employed in the work of the village settlement.

Many of the new Norman gentry, who received from the Conqueror grants of land in return for their services in helping him to conquer England, gave their names to their new possessions. Thus, the Mandevilles settled at Stoke, and called it Stoke-Mandeville; the Vernons at Minshall, and called it Minshall-Vernon; the Courtenays at Sutton, which thus became Sutton-Courtenay; the Pierponts settled at Hurst in Sussex, and called it Hurst-Pierpont, where they built their castle; the Nevilles at Holt, which became Neville-Holt; the Lisles at Kingston, and made it Kingston-Lisle; the Norris family at Hampstead in Berkshire, and converted the name of the place into Hampstead-Norris; and many other names compounded of Saxon and Norman words record the names of William's hungry followers, who received a reward at the expense of the former Saxon owners.

So the village settled down under its new owner, and possibly was fortunate enough to escape from outside disturbances. There was plenty of strife in England during Stephen's reign, when war raged between the partisans of that monarch and the Empress Maud. Lawless barons erected their castles, called "adulterine," lived a life of hunting and pillage, oppressed the people, and forced them to erect their strongholds, which were filled with "devils and evil men." Over a thousand castles were built in nineteen years, and in his own castle each earl or lord reigned as a small king, coining his own money, making his own laws, having power of life and death over his dependants, and often using his power most violently and oppressively. After an expedition against a powerful neighbour he would retire to his castle, shut himself up there, repel the vengeance of his foes, and resist the authorities who attempted to maintain order in the country. It was a happy thing for England when these adulterine castles were destroyed in the reign of Henry II., and peace descended upon an unhappy land. During his time the old antagonism between the conquered and the conquerors ceased, and Saxon and Norman were blended into one race.

Then the English nation sprang into being, a strong and vigorous race, capable of great achievement, with all its manly virtues, its powers of organisation and creation, placing reliance upon its own efforts, strong in its sturdy independence, and resolved to work out its own destinies, trusting little to foreign influences and ideas. Perhaps national movements little disturbed the life of our sequestered village, but their influence would be felt even in the remotest vale, and bring a sense of peace and happiness to the villagers.

CHAPTER X

THE VILLAGE IN THE THIRTEENTH CENTURY

The thirteenth-century village — Excommunication — Magna Charta—New methods of agriculture—Walter of Henley's *Husbandry*—The *Seneschaucie*—Grosseteste's *Rules*—Surveys—The bailiff—Seneschal-Provost—Hayward—Ploughman—Shepherd—Dairymaid—Lord of the Manor—Order at meals.

THE thirteenth century dawned fair and bright upon the village. It was a busy hive of industry. The ploughmen drove their team of oxen from morn to eve, and presently the hay and corn harvests were gathered in, and all the folk were busy at their various occupations; but itinerant hawkers brought sad news of the doings of a worthless King. The lord of the manor had been summoned by his over-lord to assemble his socmen and retainers, and join the ranks of the barons, who were compelling King John to keep his promises. The bells in their village church ceased to toll for service, and the Papal Interdict fell as a pall over the land. In consternation the villagers crowded to the church to ask the meaning of the strange silence of the bells, and with a sore heart their parson had to explain to them that he was bound to obey the Pope's decree, and could not hold a service till the Interdict was removed. And then their lord rode back in haste from Runnymede, and told them that the Charter of English liberty had been signed, and that freedom had dawned upon the distressed country. In spite of the Pope I expect the bells rang out a joyous peal to celebrate the good news, and soon the doors of the church were open, and the people heard the chanting of the cherubic hymn with glad hearts in the Holy Eucharist:

> Gloria in excelsis Deo. Et in terra pax hominibus bonæ voluntatis. Laudamus te, Benedicimus te, Adoramus te, Glorificamus te. Gratias agimus tibi propter magnam gloriam tuam. Domine Deus, Rex cœlestis, Deus Pater omnipotens. Domine Fili, unigenite Jesu Christe. . .

There was joy in the village. And the work prospered. Farming in the thirteenth century seems to have been managed with much more system and care than formerly. Four treatises on agriculture written in Norman French have come down to us from that time, and are extremely valuable in revealing the condition of a village in that period. It was then that the practice of keeping written accounts on each estate became general,[1] showing the care that was bestowed upon the management of estates. The countryside was prosperous. New markets were opened by the rise of towns, the establishment of new monasteries and the increased trade promoted by fairs, all contributed to the well-being of the rustics. Moreover, there was a greater opportunity of intercourse between village and town, and for the circulation of money. In former times the lord and his tenants would consume

[1] *Agriculture and Prices*, by Professor Thorold Rogers, i. 2

the produce of the land, or store it for future use, and not concern themselves about the outside world. Now they had begun to sell their surplus stock of corn or other commodities, and receive money payment for them. A change took place in the position of the villein. Instead of working two or three days on his lord's land every week, he paid to him some money in lieu of service, just as a modern tenant farmer pays rent for his holding. And instead of the work on the home farm being done by the compulsory service of villeins, the lord would hire labourers to carry it on. This arrangement was, doubtless, satisfactory to both parties. Forced labour can never be very strenuously performed, and the bailiff had always found it difficult to keep the villeins at their work. Ploughs would somehow always be breaking down, and they took a long time to be repaired, and the servile labourer would never hurry himself. So it suited the lord to be quit of these half-hearted villeins, and to hire men to do his farming. The arrangement also pleased the villein, as he was rid of an irksome duty, could look after his own thirty acres, make a larger profit on his land, sell his produce, and purchase more land and become a freeman and a man of some importance in the village, and not unknown in the neighbouring town where he took his produce to be sold.

The four thirteenth-century treatises to which I have referred are the following: (1) Walter of Henley's *Husbandry*. Nothing is known of the author. (2) An anonymous book entitled *Husbandry*

(3) The *Seneschaucie*, recounting the duties of the officials of the community. (4) An interesting book containing *Rules* for the management of an estate, drawn up by the good and famous Bishop of Lincoln, Robert Grosseteste, who found time, amid his many episcopal duties, to write this treatise for the Countess of Lincoln, to enable her "to guard and govern her lands and hostel." He added the pleasant assurance: "Whoever will keep these rules well will be able to live on his means, and keep himself and those belonging to him."[1]

All these documents are characterised by abundant common sense, great knowledge of farming, sometimes not a little humour, as well as piety. It is amusing to read the little homely proverbs by which Walter of Henley enforces his advice on the son who is listening to his father's counsels. Thus, he wrote:

> It is said in the proverb, "Who provides for the future enjoys himself in the present." You see some who have lands and tenements and know not how to live. Why? I will tell you. Because they live without rule and forethought, and spend and waste more than their lands are worth yearly. . . . The English proverb says, "He that stretches farther than his whittle will reach, in the straw his feet he must stretch." Dear son, be prudent in your doings and be on your guard against the world, which is so wicked and deceitful.

He advises that all the property should be carefully surveyed by true and sworn men, courts,

[1] The Royal Historical Society conferred a great assistance on all students of rural economy by publishing their four treatises, which were transcribed and translated by Elizabeth Lamond, with an introduction by Archdeacon Cunningham.

gardens, dove-houses,[1] curcilages, acres in demesne, and all the estate. The survey shall state how much every item is worth, and also the amount of land held by the free tenants and by what service, and by the customary tenants and by what service. "And let customs be put in money," he adds, showing that it was advisable for the lord to release his tenants from bond work, receiving in lieu thereof a monetary payment. He gives minute directions about ploughing, and says that a horse or ox must be a poor beast which cannot from the morning go easily in pace three leagues in length from the starting-place, and return by 3 o'clock.

The bailiff, messer, or provost, was a very important official, who was elected by the tenants; he had to work very hard overseeing the ploughmen, keeping the customary servants, who were often neglectful, to their work, and preventing fraud. An ox team with two horses was better than a horse team, inasmuch as the horse costs more to keep. Each horse had to be kept in the stall from St. Luke's Day to Holy Cross Day in May (time was always then reckoned by the feast days in the Kalendar), and required one-sixth part of a bushel of oats—price one halfpenny—and at least twelve pennyworth of grass in summer, and a penny a week in shoeing. Our modern farmers would like to feed their nags so cheaply.

I have no space to record Walter of Henley's directions with regard to sowing—though I may

[1] Manor-lords and high ecclesiastics were alone permitted to have pigeon-cotes.

Bailiff directing the Labours of Reapers

mention that he was wise enough to advocate a change of seed, "for seed grown on other ground will bring more profit than that which is grown on your own"—draining, the keeping and preparing manure, the inspecting of cattle. Worldly wisdom is scattered over Walter's pages: "Know for a truth that bad beasts cost more than good ones." Buy cattle between Easter and Whitsuntide, for then beasts are spare and cheap. Change your horses before they are too old and worn out, for with little money you can rear good and young ones, if you sell and buy in season. It is well to know how one ought to keep cattle to teach your people, for when they see that you understand it, they will take the more pains to do well. Moreover, we learn how much milk the cows should yield. Ewes were milked as well as cows. Thirty ewes yielded as much butter and cheese as three cows did. He gives four rules for servants who have the goods of others in their keeping: To love their lord and respect him; and as to making profit, they ought to look on the business as their own; and as to outlays, they ought to think that the business is another's. These thirteenth-century ideas are quite as applicable to the twentieth; but then, as now, many neglected the first three, and only observed the fourth.

The *Seneschaucie* is, perhaps, the most useful of the four treatises in furnishing a picture of village life in the thirteenth century. The lord's chief official was the seneschal or steward who, two or three times a year, made his rounds and visited the manors of his stewardshire, inquired into the rents, services, and customs, and at his first coming caused the lands to be measured, and made himself acquainted with all the agricultural details of the estate. He had to inquire into the conduct of the bailiff and his subordinate officers, prevent trespass, waste, and destruction, and promote the interests of the lord in every way.

The head official on the estate was the bailiff, who was required to be faithful and a good husbandman, and had many responsible duties. In fact, it is difficult to understand how one man could perform all the multitudinous duties that devolved upon him. He was required to rise early every morning and survey the woods, corn, meadows, and pastures, see the ploughs yoked and unyoked, the land marked and manured, and supervise the work of tenants, to see how many acres of corn were sowed and reaped, and how the horses and oxen and sheep were kept. He could not trespass upon the duties of the steward by taking fines, nor bake or brew without warrant from the lord. He had to be just and honest himself, and see that all the people were honest also. The surplus of the farm was to be sold in fair or market. The guarding of horses and beasts from accident, the shearing and selling of the wool, and the conduct of the shepherds required his attention. The cocks and sheaves of corn were to be kept small, so that they should dry the quicker, and the small sheaf was better for loading, stacking, and threshing. I cannot tell you half of the duties that fell to the lot of this overworked individual.

MARCH: LOPPING TREES

(From a *Shepherd's Calendar*, British Museum, fourteenth century)

Under the bailiff was the provost, who was elected by the common consent of the village as the best husbandman. He seems to have been a kind of under-bailiff, and besides seeing to the yoking of the plough-teams he had to provide folds for welters, ewes, and hogs, to see that the threshing was done well and thoroughly, prevent dishonesty, searching the threshers and winnowers lest they should carry away any corn in their bosoms, tunic, boots, pockets, sacks, or sacklets. The agricultural labourers in those days lacked not supervision.

Another official was the hayward, who was required to be an active and sharp man, working early and late, inspecting the woods, corn, and meadows, superintending the ploughers and harrowers, and seeing that the tenants did their boon-work on the lord's land. In haytime and harvest he was very busy looking after the mowers and reapers, and seeing that his lord suffered no loss. There were auditors, also, who attended to the business of rents and outlays and the returns of the grange and stock, and checked the accounts of the steward, bailiff, and provost, who had to present these to them for their inspection.

The ploughmen were required to be men of intelligence, and to be able to repair broken ploughs and harrows, to till the land well, and to know how to yoke and drive oxen without beating or hurting them, and how to feed them well. To the ploughman belonged the duty of draining the land by making ditches. They were specially cautioned not to take fire into the byre for light or

JUNE: SHEEP-SHEARING

(From a *Shepherd's Calendar*, British Museum, fourteenth century)

warmth, nor a candle, unless it were in a lantern. The waggoner had to take great care of the horses, and to curry them, not to overload, overwork, or overdrive or hurt them, and to know how to mend the harness. He was required to sleep every night with his horses, the oxherds with their oxen, and the cowherd with his cows. The swineherd kept his pigs in the forest, or in woods or waste land, or in marshes. During hard frost he made sties for them, and the sows after farrowing, and feeble ones he drove into the home farm of the manor, and fed them with leavings so long as the cold weather lasted.

The shepherd is much the same in all periods, and his mode of keeping his charges in the thirteenth century differs little from his duties to-day. The shepherd and his dog are familiar figures in the English landscape. He was required to cover his fold, and enclose with hurdles which he made with his own hands; and to guard his flock, lest the sheep should be killed by dogs or stolen. The shepherd's recreations are disclosed by the order that he must not leave his sheep to go to fairs, or markets, or wrestling matches, or wakes, to which I hope to refer later on. The dairymaid was an important person, who was required to be faithful and of good repute, and to keep herself clean and to know her business. She made cheese and salt cheese and butter, and had to winnow the corn, to look after the geese and hens and capons, and all the small animals, such as sucking pigs and peacocks. Sows were expected to farrow twice a year, having at

JULY: MOWING

(From a *Shepherd's Calendar*, British Museum, fourteenth century)

each time seven pigs, and each goose five goslings, and each hen, for one hundred and fifteen eggs, seven chickens, three of which were to be made capons. All kinds of minute details are given, so that the farmer had no lack of information with regard to his business, and the present-day agriculturist might learn much from these thirteenth-century directions.

The duties of the lord of the manor are set forth as clearly as those of his servants. He is to examine the accounts of the auditors and the conduct of the steward, bailiff, and provost, to hear the complaints and wrongs of any servant who has suffered by the misconduct of his officials; and, finally:

> The lord ought to love God and justice, and be faithful and true in his sayings and doings; and he ought to hate sin and injustice and evil-doing. The lord ought not to take counsel with young men full of young blood and ready courage, who know little or nothing of business, nor of any juggler, flatterer, or idle talker, nor of such as bear witness by present; but he ought to take counsel with worthy and faithful men, ripe in years, who have seen much and know much, and who are known to be of good fame, and who never were caught or convicted for treachery or any wrong-doing; nor for love, nor for hate, nor for fear, nor for menace, nor for gain, nor for loss, will turn aside from truth, and knowingly counsel their lord to do him harm.

Very excellent advice! Let us hope that the lord usually followed it. The *Rules* of the good bishop, Robert Grosseteste, which he kindly made for the guidance of the Countess of Lincoln with regard to the lord's duties, are very full and minute.

AUGUST: REAPING

(From a *Shepherd's Calendar*, British Museum, fourteenth century)

They show that this excellent prelate was as good a farmer as he was a theologian. He advocated a sort of patriarchal government of the estate. The lord should exhort all his household to serve God and himself faithfully and painstakingly, and should see that all the servants should be faithful, painstaking, chaste, clean, honest, and profitable. I regret that the limits of space prevent me from dwelling further upon the Bishop's sound and good advice. Grosseteste led rather a stormy life. He had a vast diocese to superintend, extending from the Humber to the Thames. He had to fight controversial battles, with his own dean and chapter, and against the Pope, who suspended him for refusing to institute an Italian into an English benefice; and doubtless he found some relaxation in devising these excellent *Rules* for the benefit of the Countess and all good English landlords.

One other point may be alluded to, and that is the order and decency of behaviour in the hall at meal-times. Dinner was served with much formality and decorum, both with regard to the seating of the company and the serving of the meal. The Bishop directed:

Make your freemen and guests sit as far as possible at tables on either side, nor four here and three there. And all the crowd of grooms shall enter together when the freemen are seated, and shall sit together and rise together. And strictly forbid that any quarrelling be at your meals. And you yourself always be seated at the middle of the high table, that your presence as lord or lady may appear openly to all, and that you plainly see on either side all the service and all the faults. And be careful of this, that each day at your meals you have two overseers over your household when you sit at meals, and of this be sure, that you shall be very much feared and reverenced.

The Countess was bidden, in spite of sickness or fatigue, to constrain herself to eat in the hall before her people, " for this shall bring great benefit and honour to you." Grace was said by the chaplain, and before it with much formality the pantry-keeper with the bread and the butler with the cup came to the high table, and three varlets were ordered to serve the high table and the tables of the freemen with drink. Ale vessels were kept under the table, and wine only placed upon it. No dispute, noise, or bad words were allowed. At each course the servers went into the kitchen and, headed by the steward, brought the dishes to the high table; and then to the carvers at the other tables. It was all arranged " decently and in order."

The thirteenth century has been called the Golden Age of English Churchmanship. It was a century of high ideals and earnest faith. The men who were building our churches were fired by lofty aspirations, and wrought wonderful things, seeking after light with glowing aspiration. The men wrought well and worthily. During the century there was sore fighting on English land, but the village life went on usually undisturbed by the conflict of King and barons, and agriculture improved and the people prospered.

CHAPTER XI

THE PEASANTS' REVOLT IN THE FOURTEENTH CENTURY

The fourteenth-century village—Increased freedom—*The Vision of Piers Plowman*—Age of military glory—Rise of wages—Black Death—Rural exodus—Statute of Labourers—General discontent—The Lollards—John Ball—Peasants' Rising—Kentish disturbances and in East Anglia—Their failure.

WHEN the fourteenth century dawned the social conditions of the village were pleasanter than in the preceding period. There was more freedom, as John Barbour sang:

> Ah! Freedom is a noble thing!
> Freedom mayde man to have liking (liberty);
> Freedom all solace to man gives;
> He lives at ease that freely lives!

Customs of manors requiring forced labour had become changed into payments for toil in money or kind. The villein paid a rent for his farm instead of his boon-service. When labour was scarce sometimes the bailiff would try to return to the old system, and there were disputes and contentions that marred the peace of the village. Everywhere there was a desire for greater freedom. Industrial unrest, which forms such a feature of modern life, was manifesting itself in the busy towns, as well as in the most secluded hamlets. As we look back, it is not difficult to discover the causes of the perturbation.

The wonderful poem of William Langland, entitled "The Vision of Piers Plowman," that he saw on a May morning sleeping by a burnside on the Malvern Hills, gives a striking picture of his time, as he marshals his various characters, his lords and ladies, priests and hermits, minstrels and jugglers, and beggars and rustic ploughmen who, "in setting and sowing swonken (toil) full hard." His homely truths and pithy sayings would be borne by the ballad-singers into the villages, and arouse the imagination of the peasants, and kindle greater desire for freedom; though "Long Will" was very impartial in his denunciation of abuses, and while he bade lords to "do justice and love mercy," he did not spare the idle husbandman; and while he scoffed at unworthy ministers, religion was to him a very real thing—"For religion, in reason, hath somewhat for certain," and religion had begun somewhat to decline. The time of ardent hope had passed. The autumn of the Middle Ages had set in.

He told the lord that he must not wrest gifts from his tenants, nor misdo the poor. "Though he be thy underling here, well may hap in heaven that he be worthier set, and with greater bliss than thou. For in charnel at church churles be evil to know, or a knight from a knave there." Again he sings in the same strain: "Beguile not thy bondman, the better thou'll speed; though under thee here, it may happen in heaven his seat may be higher, in saintlier bliss." Though preaching an equality in God's sight, he recognised the distinction of class and proclaimed the gospel of labour. The aim of Piers the Ploughman was to work and to make the world work with him. He warns the labourer as well as the lord. Hunger is God's instrument in bringing the idlest to toil, and Hunger waits to work her will on the idler and the waster. He advocates fair wages, and says of the "landless labourers that live by their hands, that they must highly be hired or else they will chide." Seeing the dearth of labourers, he advises them to make the most of their present opportunities:

> I warn you, ye workmen, to win while ye may;
> For hunger now hitherwards hastens full fast.

But "Long Will" set his face against revolt, which he tried to avert. However, the circumstances of the time were too strong for him. The reign of Edward III. was a period of war and of military glory. Creçy and Poictiers were won by the gallantry of English bowmen, the men of the village and town who had practised their archery at the country butts. The Scottish wars were continuous, and men from the village swelled the ranks of the fighters, and diminished the number of labourers. The value of labour increased and wages rose. And then that hideous pall fell upon Europe and England —the Black Death. Modern research has shown that the reports of its ravages were by no means exaggerated. Something like one-half of the

SEPTEMBER: GATHERING FRUIT AND PRESSING GRAPES

(From *a Shepherd's Calendar*, British Museum, fourteenth century)

population died. The results were appalling. The land became derelict. "The sheep and cattle strayed through the fields and cornlands, and there were none left that could drive them." Few of the clergy were left alive in the villages; few services could be held, and religion lost some of its hold on the people—at least, for a time. As the century progressed the country somewhat recovered from the awful calamity. There do not exist many Churchwardens' Accounts earlier than the fifteenth century, but those that remain bear witness to the activities of the Church. The Accounts of Hedon, Yorkshire, date back to 1370, and are of great and exceptional interest. They record money collected on the fair day and Holy Cross day, when the relics were exhibited, from the offertory boxes placed in front of the Holy Cross and the image of Our Lady, and on Sundays. The Accounts of St. Nicholas' Church record the erection of a rood-screen in 1379. The Tavistock Accounts record the repair of several windows, the buying of wax for candles. But these concern large and important churches in towns, and not village churches, of which no fourteenth-century Churchwardens' Accounts are extant. The next century will furnish far more material from this source.

The ravages of the Black Death, which began in 1348, entailed some alarming results. The population of England at that time was only between three and four millions, and it can easily be imagined how the deaths of half this number of people made agricultural and other labour almost impossible.

OCTOBER: PLOUGHING, SOWING, AND THRESHING

(From a *Shepherd's Calendar*, British Museum, fourteenth century)

Again wages rose, and prices of food rose too; and with it the antagonism between capital and labour began to rear its hideous head, as it has done in times less remote.

A sort of rural exodus began. Labourers wandered away from the village to seek higher wages elsewhere. Owing to the deaths of so many tenants, the lord had much additional land on his hands, which the surviving tenants were glad enough to acquire; and later on they waxed rich over the bargain. As they could not get labourers, they increased their flocks of sheep. But the country had many landless men roaming about who could obtain work if they listed; but they often preferred the wild life of the woods, and to become bandits and beggars and plundering travellers. The state of the country moved the Government to action, and the Statute of Labourers, passed in 1349, was the result. It ran as follows:

> Every man or woman of whatsoever condition, free or bond, able in body and within the age of threescore years, and not having of his own whereof he may live, nor land of his own about the tillage of which he may occupy himself, and not serving any other, shall be bound to serve the employer who shall require him to do so, and shall take only the wages which were accustomed to be taken in the neighbourhood where he is bound to serve.

If a man refused to obey this law he was sent to prison. But that was not all. Little improvement in the state was wrought. So two years later the Government made a further attack upon the liberties of the subject. It revived the old law, tying each man to his own village, and declaring that anyone who tried to escape was a fugitive and liable to fine and imprisonment. Later on the order was made that such runaway labourers should be branded on the forehead with a hot iron. Stewards in want of labourers revoked the deeds of exemption which villeins had bought with hard money, and endeavoured to revive all the old customary services that had long been abandoned.

In consequence of these hard laws the country was seething with discontent. Villeins who had become rich supported the claims of the labourers, and cries of fierce anger resounded through the land. The Lollards, too, were preaching unsettling doctrines, questioning the authority of the Church and advocating the cause of social equality. The elements of strife, confusion, and revolution were present everywhere; and only awaited a few ardent leaders to sound the bugle call to arms. Such a leader was John Ball, a Kentish priest, who uttered the first notes of defiance to authority, and preached that all men were equal, and that every man had his rights. He advocated a community of goods, and the abolition of all distinction between a villein and a gentleman. All men were equal, and as he preached the doctrines of extreme socialism to crowds assembled in each village churchyard, he sounded forth the familiar refrain which was caught up and echoed on throughout the country—

When Adam delved and Eve span,
Who was then the gentleman ?

If we all come from the same father and mother, of Adam and Eve, how can these lords prove that they are better than we, if it be not that they make us gain for them by our toil what they spend in their pride? They are clothed in velvet, and warm in their furs and ermines, while we are covered with rags. They have wine and spices and fair bread; and we oat-cake and straw, and water to drink. They have leisure and fine houses; we have pain and labour, the rain and the winds in the fields. And yet it is of us and our toil that these men hold their state.

Such was John Ball's preaching. It fired the minds of the people and stirred their imagination. They swore to resist these miserable new laws. Nothing would induce them to obey them. For the first time there was a real bitter antagonism between the upper and lower ranks of society, and class war and hatred were only awaiting a spark to kindle the alarming flame. This spark was the levying of a hateful poll-tax of 1s. in 1380 upon every person in the kingdom, no matter how low his status. Every labourer was required to pay one shilling out of his wages, and the fire spread from village to village. The Peasants' Rising was no hastily planned movement. It was a carefully planned campaign to redress the evils of long standing, and to rebel against the King and his councillors "for making such laws, labourers to grieve," as Piers Plowman said. A long time before the Rising a rumour ran through the country of a "Great Society," which called upon the working people to rise as one man and break the yoke of bondage. Quaint rhymes were issued by the leaders, and found their way into remote villages, summoning the peasants to fight for their freedom. This is one of the curious appeals:

John Schep, some time Saint Mary's priest of York, and now of Colchester, greeteth well John Nameless and John the Miller and John Carter, and biddeth them that they beware of guile in borough, and stand together in God's name, and biddeth Piers Plowman go to his work and chastise well Hobb the Robber, and take with him John Trueman and all his fellows and no mo; and look sharp you to one-head (union) and no mo.

John Miller hath aground small, small, small.
The King's son of heaven shall pay for all.
Be ware or ye be wo (worse)
Know your friend from your foe.
Have enough and say "Ho!" (stop)
And do well and better and flee sin,
And seek peace and hold therein.
And so bid John Trueman and all his fellows.

The Kentish insurgent sent forth his missive. "John Ball greeteth you all, and doth for to understand he hath rung your bell. Now right and might, will and skill, God speed every dele." Each county has its story of the events that happened. Kent was the earliest scene of the revolt, and one of the earliest acts was the seizure of the house of William Medmenham, probably a steward of various manors, where the insurgents burnt all the Court Rolls and books. "John Rakestraw" and "Watte the Tegheler of Essex," otherwise Wat Tyler, seized William de Septvanz, the sheriff, whose books and rolls were burned. John Ball was a prisoner in

Canterbury Castle when the rebellion commenced. Him and other prisoners they released, and then took vengeance on numerous persons obnoxious to them. Some were murdered; others put to ransom; and the houses of Sir Thomas Fog and others were plundered of goods valued at a thousand pounds. They mustered in strong force at Blackheath on June 13; on the 14th Archbishop Sudbury was murdered, and on the 15th Wat Tyler was slain at Smithfield by the Lord Mayor's dagger. This blow did not end the revolt, as, although the rebels retreated from London, they carried on their war for some months, and one, Henry Aleyn, headed a very destructive band round Canterbury for some months.

Perhaps the most formidable revolt was in East Anglia, where divers motives caused the trouble. In East Norfolk the peasants shared the opinions of their fellows in Kent and elsewhere, and the revolt was mainly political. In West Norfolk the peasants had no great grievance, but they waged a real class war. They were in search of plunder, and the unpopular persons of the ruling class were the objects of their furious animosity. These were the nobility, the regular clergy (*i.e.*, the abbots and monks), and the lawyers. The lesser secular clergy, the rectors, and vicars, seem to have sided with the peasants, and were often their leaders. Another obnoxious class were the foreign weavers who had been invited to England by Edward III. from Flanders in order to improve the making of English cloth. Naturally the English weavers disliked these foreigners, who seemed to be taking the bread out of English mouths. They regarded them as the modern Trade Unionist does a "black-leg," especially as these foreigners kept the secrets of their trade to themselves. Hence the weavers took the opportunity of the revolt to make a clean sweep of these obnoxious Flemings, especially at King's Lynn.[1] Bands of armed rustics roamed the country, pillaging and destroying and murdering; Court Rolls were everywhere destroyed. Their chief leader was one Geoffrey Lyster of Felmingham. There was also a John Lytstere, who called himself the "King of the Commons." He and his rebels captured some knights, and this "King" made them wait upon him with bent knee as he sat at meat.

I need not follow the course of the revolt, which extended to many parts of the country. It was met in Norfolk vigorously by the stalwart fighting bishop, Henry le Despencer, of Norwich, who, by powerful military action, captured and beheaded the ringleaders and subdued the rebels, showing little mercy. But generally throughout the country the law seems to have been enforced fairly and justly, and at the end of the year a general amnesty was proclaimed. The Rising proved itself a hopeless failure. Its leaders were slain or fugitives, and it accomplished nothing. It brought much

[1] A very full and interesting account of the Norfolk Rising has recently been published by Christobel M. Hoare (Mrs. Ivo Hood) in her book, *The History of an East Anglian Soke*, to which the reader is referred.

misery to the countryside. It arrested the movement towards freedom that had been going on for a century at least. It riveted chains that had well-nigh been broken. It united the knights and lords in their struggle against the labourers, and destroyed the ancient harmony that had existed between the various classes of the community. It brought forth reactionary legislation. Boroughs were ordered to send back to the manors any runaway villeins. Boon-services were again enforced, and in 1388 children above the age of twelve years were ordered not to leave their native village, or to be educated, lest they should go to one of the Universities and seek Holy Orders. The results seem to have been lamentably small for so great an effort, but it really accomplished much. The villein had still to work his accustomed days on the lord's land, and submit to certain fretting and galling conditions. But he had shown his lord that he was a person of some importance, that he could combine with his fellows and form insurrections, if he so pleased; and, consequently, that he was a man who had to be reckoned with, who had certain rights that could not be infringed or disregarded; and his own ruined house and burnt Court Rolls bore witness to the power of the British peasant when once he was aroused. However, the country had had enough of fighting, and the village had peace.

An extraordinarily valuable picture of village life in the fourteenth century is shown in the *Louttrel Psalter*, which was produced about 1330. Archbishop Chichele had issued an order that every

NOVEMBER: PREPARING WINTER STORES

(From a *Shepherd's Calendar*, British Museum, fourteenth century)

parish should provide a Psalter for use in the church. This was rather a serious matter, as Sir George Louttrel, rector of Irnham, found to his cost. So he consulted his squire, who happened to be a relative, Sir Robert Louttrel, who at once said, "I will do it, and it shall be a good one." So he had this famous book inscribed and illustrated. It consists of three hundred and nine leaves, and was illuminated in gold and silver and other colours by one man, who was a consummate artist and keen observer and lacked

WOMEN MILKING EWES (FROM THE "LOUTTREL PSALTER")

(From Hone's *Manor and Manorial Records*)

not humour. It illustrates most wonderfully life in England in the fourteenth century. We seem to hear the cart-wheels groaning beneath the heavily laden cart, and to see the dragon-fly flashing past us like a flash of light. Pilgrimages were in full blast, and a boat is bearing a full cargo to the shrine of St. James in Spain. We see the pedlar plying his trade like a Shakespearian Autolycus, and the tinker and the tooth-drawer busily engaged. Criminals are flying to sound the sanctuary knocker, and so to save their skins. Itinerant mountebanks make their way from village to village. There is the pole-holder, the stilt-walker, the woman dancing like Salome, and the conjurer amusing and mystifying the people by his tricks. Sports and pastimes appear largely, including the bear fight, knights fighting in tournaments, and the *château d'amour*, a huge machine that was wheeled into the arena full of fair maidens, who challenge the knights to combat. The artist's pictures of agriculture are most illuminating. We see the rustics ploughing, while others break the clods of earth with mallets, sowing, cutting thistles, harrowing, reaping, threshing. The sheep in the folds are being milked; a goose-boy is driving goslings. Boys will be boys in all ages, and here some boy is stealing cherries. These are some of the wondrous paintings that fill the book, which makes the dead past live again, and reflects very closely the scenes of rural life in the fourteenth century.

CHAPTER XII

THE VILLAGE IN THE FIFTEENTH CENTURY

Wars of the Roses—The Lollards—Jack Cade—Growth of liberty—Improved agriculture—Sheep-farming—Weaving and spinning wool—Authority of the clergy—Penance—Church services—Churchwardens—Relief of the poor—Sidesmen or questmen—Parish clerk—Chantries—Origin of vicarages—Tithes—Bell-ringer—Guilds—Parish feasts—Church house—Church ales—Village gaiety—Pilgrimages.

THE political events of the fifteenth century do not concern us very closely in our secluded village, but upon many public and State affairs pressed heavily. Civil war raged. The Wars of the Roses brought suffering and misery to many homes; but the fighting was not continuous, and only here and there battles were fought. Except when the armies of the great lords passed through the village, the life of the community was not much disturbed. Within sight of the fierce fighting of belted earls and stalwart bowmen, the sturdy ploughman continued to turn his even furrow, though young men of the village caught the martial fever, rushed to the standard of the "Kingmaker," Warwick, or of one of his opponents, and sought a life of freedom and adventure.

Moreover, the peasants fought also. The fifteenth century was not an era of universal peace

Under the leadership of Lord Cobham the Lollards stirred up a rebellion early in the century; and the county of Kent was agitated in 1450 by the insurrection of Jack Cade, or "Mortimer," though this was not of a democratic character, but was supported by men of position, including a knight, eighteen squires, and seventy-four gentlemen of the shire, and several clergymen. It was directed against the extortions practised by the King's officers. History books record the progress of the revolt, and tell how its unfortunate leader was captured near Lewes, taken prisoner, wounded in a struggle, and died on the road to London. However, this would not disturb the peace of other shires. Plague and famine, however, did bring misery to many hamlets, and during the years that preceded the Reformation many changes took place in their social and economic life.

In the last chapter we saw that the Peasants' Revolt was practically a failure, and that it ended in riveting the chains of serfdom that had been well-nigh broken, and hindering the growth of freedom. In the fifteenth century, however, the growth of liberty progressed. A better feeling between the manor lords and their tenants sprang into being, and the growth of prosperity increased this. When we considered the curious method of farming that existed in England, the scattered strips in the common fields, we must have realised that the arrangement was far from being economical. At last it seemed to have dawned upon the villagers, and they and the lord decided that it was capable of improvement. So they set to work to rearrange the land by a system of exchange of these several strips, enclosing the new portions within fences, and thus forming small farms and holdings, instead of the scattered bits of land in different parts of the common fields. Moreover, sheep-farming progressed rapidly. There was a great demand for English wool in foreign markets, and for English cloth also. English wool was considered to be the best in the world, and the methods of making cloth, improved by the advent of industrious Flemings, had established a great reputation in foreign markets. So a new industry arose. In the villages and towns, especially in East Anglia, in the north of England, and also in the southern counties, weaving and spinning went on merrily. Large weaving factories, such as that of Jack of Newbury in Berkshire, were established, employing a great number of hands, and every Monday morning packhorses were ridden into the country villages with stocks of wool for the peasants to spin, bringing back the work of the preceding week. All this brought much gain to the villagers and prosperity to the village. The sun seemed to smile on rural England, and all was well.

Let us visit the village and see how the people lived. The Church played a great part in the life of the village community. Religion and social life were blended together very closely. The Sunday services—Matins, Mass, and Evensong—were well attended. "Piers Plowman" states that after working on weekdays, and the lords hunting the fox and other beasts in the wild woods,

And upon Sunday to cease, God's service to hear,
Both Matins and Masse, and after meat in churches
To hear their Evensong, every man ought.

The clergy exercised great authority over the people, and the churchwardens were required to present those who neglected their religious duties, and these were punished in the Ecclesiastical Courts. Persons were sentenced to do penance for working on Sundays or Saints' Days. They had to walk in front of the procession in church on Sundays as penitents, receive two fustigations or beatings with a staff, and pay a fine. Mass was celebrated at 9 a.m., and was preceded by Matins. Few communicated except at Easter, but bits of the "holy loaf" were passed round as I have seen in a Normandy church at the present day. Evensong was said at 3 p.m. Afterwards they played at games, even in the churchyard. In times not remote the parson at Downham, near Clitheroe in Lancashire, used to "kick off" the football after afternoon service. On weekdays there were services. In Peckham's *Constitutions* every priest was directed to say Mass once a week, but later on celebrations were more frequent, and in large churches the three services were said daily. In the country people were content with a service on Wednesday and Friday. Saints' Days were like Sundays, and were holidays. No work was done; and as these days were far more numerous than in our calendar the rustic was not without leisure. Sermons were preached occasionally, but by no means at every service. The "Bidding Prayer" was regarded with much reverential affection. It asked the prayers of the congregation for all high personages in Church and State, including the Pope and his Cardinals, the parson of the parish, for the worshippers, for benefactors, such as the givers of lights, wax, lands, etc.; for parishioners travelling, for sinners and for the good, for the sick, for regular tithe-payers, for pilgrims, for the fruits of the earth, for women labouring with child, for the souls of dear ones departed, and for those in purgatory. A Bede Roll was kept containing the names of those who had recently died, which were read out and prayers asked for them. The Litany was chanted in procession round the church, the people chanting after every clause *Ora pro nobis*.

The churchwardens were very important people. They date back to the thirteenth century, and in the fifteenth were appointed by the parishioners annually at a parish meeting. All the adults in the village had a voice in the election. They had to keep careful accounts of the expenditure during their year of office, and hand over to their successors any balance there might be. Their duties were very responsible. People used to make gifts in kind to the church, such as lands, houses, flocks, and herds, cows, and hives of bees. All these had to be cared for by the wardens. The fabric of the church, except the chancel, which belonged to the rector, had to be kept in repair, together with the churchyard and the church house; and they had charge of all the church treasures, the vestments, furniture, bells, and everything else. All these were the property of the parish, and the wardens, as their representatives, had them in their keeping. If new furniture was required the people provided it. And their duties did not end there. They had to care for the poor. There was a common chest, out of which they relieved the sick, or those who had need of relief by loans without interest. Cows were kept to provide milk for them. A good man left four cows to his parish to be let at a rent, the proceeds to pay for the "paschal light." Many of the early wardens' accounts have come down to us, and these show the life and extraordinary activity of the village, and how willing men were always ready to devote their time and influence to the managements of its affairs. They reveal also the simplicity of the population, the cheerful contentment, the general absence of fraud, their religious feelings and general goodwill towards each other. Once a year the wardens attended the archdeacon's Visitation Court, and were obliged to present the names of any who had been guilty of moral offences.

In this matter they were helped by the sidesmen. Few people seem to know the origin of this office, and suppose that whereas the duty of the wardens was to collect the offerings of the faithful in the nave, the sidesmen performed a like duty in the side aisles. The name is a corruption of synodsmen,[1] the men who attended the diocesan synod. They were also called questmen, and their duty

[1] Some doubt has been thrown upon this derivation. The late Professor Skeat pronounced against it; but it does not seem to be an impossible corruption.

was to answer a set of questions with regard to their parson, the parishioners, and the condition of the church. These questions number sixty-eight, and are of a most minute and inquisitorial character. The reputation of the rectors is usually excellent; but some faults are found occasionally. One vicar is reported to preach after his own fashion; and although he expounded the Gospels as far as he knew, he did not teach them much about the Articles of the Faith, the Commandments, and the mortal sins. He was accused of incontinence, and did not keep his house in repair. Another vicar, though a good man, only preached as far as he knew, but not sufficiently. He disliked the friars whom his predecessor welcomed, and would not suffer them to preach in his church or welcome them to his house. Such were some of the complainings of discontented parishioners. It will be gathered that the wardens and sidesmen had no light tasks during their year of office. I have been publishing the churchwardens' accounts of St. Mary's, Thame, during its rebuilding, and the care with which they were drawn up, and the volume of them, serve as a model for all time.

Another important official was the parish clerk, whose story I have told in another book.[1] He was a very busy person, his duties being to attend upon the rector and assist in the services; to ring the bell, prepare the altar, lead the people in the responses, precede the procession with holy water, and when the priest visited the sick he led the way, carrying

[1] *The Parish Clerk*, by P. H. Ditchfield, fourth edition (Methuen).

a bell and a candle. On Sunday and great festivals he used to go round the parish, enter the houses, and sprinkle the inhabitants with holy water. Sometimes he taught the children of the village, and the office was often a stepping-stone to higher preferment in the Church and to Holy Orders. Every one knows Chaucer's description of a parish clerk, who was a townsman and of a gay and volatile nature, and did not very closely resemble the quiet, sober, and dignified official who performed his manifold duties in the village church. He received regular wages once a quarter, sometimes had a house provided for him with some land to cultivate, a present from families of a loaf at Easter, and some eggs, and some of the farmers' corn at harvest-time.

HOLY WATER CLERK
(From Gasquet's *Parish Life in Mediæval England*)

In many old churches we find a chantry, which was served by a priest duly appointed for that purpose. The chantry was often founded by the squire or lord of the manor, and prayers and masses were offered daily for the souls of the founder, his relatives, and his friends. The chantry-priest was a very useful addition to the clerical staff, and, as at Wokingham, he acted also as the master of a grammar school. In town churches there were, of course, many other church officials, deacons, and sub-deacons; but in our village the vicar or rector sufficed. The origin of vicarages is well known. When some generous lord founded a monastery he often assigned to it the advowson of some livings of which he was patron, and a portion of the tithe for its support. The monastery thus became the rector of the parish, and appointed one of the community to act as *vicarius*, or vicar—that is,

BLESSING OF FOOD BY HOLY WATER CLERK
(From Gasquet's *Parish Life in Mediæval England*)

one who acted in place of the rector. Monks made indifferent parish priests, and objection was taken to this arrangement, until at length by the Lateran Council of 1179 it was forbidden for monks to receive tithes from laymen, and the bishops were ordered to make proper provision for these appropriated parishes. Hence monasteries were forbidden from sending a monk to do duty in the vicarages, and were required to appoint a good clergyman who could not be removed at the will of the monks, and was only answerable to his bishop. For his stipend he received the small tithes—*i.e.*, the tithes of every kind except corn—and also offerings and fees, while the great tithes—*i.e.*, the tithes on corn—went to the monastery. It was not a very good arrangement, and efforts were made by Bishop Grosseteste of Lincoln and others to rescue livings from the hands of the monasteries, but in vain. To the present day the Church has suffered from this cause. At the Reformation, when the monasteries were dissolved, the great tithes owned by them were granted or sold to laymen, the *nouveaux riches*, who profited by their spoliation. More than three millions of tithe are now in the hands of laymen, and the Church has been impoverished ever since.

But to return to our village. In the times of which I am writing, another important church official was the bell-ringer, who not only rang the bell for services and for deaths and funerals, but also acted as village or town-crier, going round the parish ringing his hand-bell to summon the people to a special service of a guild, or to pray for the soul of some deceased parishioner on the monthly or yearly anniversary of his death.

And here I may tell of the very important part the guilds played in the life of the village. It is a large subject, and would require several volumes for its complete elucidation. Guilds are very ancient, and date back to Saxon times. They were of two kinds, trade guilds and religious guilds; but practically both kinds were deeply imbued with religious spirit. Although the trade guilds were founded to promote the welfare of the particular trades, such as the City Companies of London, they were deeply religious. They had their patron saint; the members met together for worship and supported a chaplain; they practised true charity, helping their brethren in distress, honouring their funerals, and praying for their souls. Religion was the guiding spirit of both. In these modern days of Poor Law (usually very poor law), Trades Unions, Benefit Societies, County Council Schools, and general materialism, religion has no part, or a very subordinate part. In former days mutual assistance, the aid of the poor, the helpless, the sick, of strangers, pilgrims, and prisoners, the burial of the dead, the keeping of schools, or of bridges and highways, were all deemed part of Christian charity, and formed part of the work the guilds set themselves to perform. The full development of guild-life belonged to towns where it was fully organised, and every kind of guild contributed to the religious and social life of the place. With these it is beyond the purpose of this book to deal. But in many villages there were guilds. We hear of the "Plowman's Light" that was kept burning before the altar of the ploughman's guild; or the village guild drew neighbours together, promoted good fellowship, encouraged charity, cared for the wants of any who had fallen into distress or sickness, and arranged and carried out amusements and festivities. Professor Thorold Rogers stated that the treasurers of the village guild used to render an accurate and annual statement to the members of their fraternity, as a bailiff did to his lord. "It is quite certain that the town and country guilds obviated pauperism in the Middle Ages, assisted in steadying the price of labour, and formed a permanent centre for those associations which fulfilled the function that in more recent times trade unions have striven to satisfy."

Where did the money come from? The members used to pay a small annual subscription. No one knew whether his goods might not be destroyed by fire or flood, or stolen by robbers, or whether he might fall ill or need a loan from the common store, or a dowry for his daughter. So all were willing to pay their annual sum. Moreover, the guild from time to time received gifts and bequests. It had a store of a few cows or sheep, which were farmed at a profit. At the beginning of this period one William Trenouth, of St. Cleer, Cornwall, left to the store of St. Cleer three sheep; to the store of St. Mary in St. Cleer Church two sheep, and the same to the store of St. James. On the feast of the Patron Saint of the Guild the members attended the church, heard Mass, and the rector preached to them a sermon. Then followed the annual feast in the church house, where they had a store of pots and pans, and pewter plates or wooden platters. These were usually the bequests of former members. Someone left his best brass pot to the Guild of St. Peter in the church of Littlebury in Essex, and also 26s. 8d. for the fraternity of Our Lady's Assumption in the church of Haddiscoe, Norfolk, for buying land and building of a hall for the guild. The Trinity Guild at Chich St. Osyth had a goodly supply of brass pots, spits, and pewter plates.

The church house was the centre of guild life.

CHURCH HOUSE, LINCOLN

(From Gasquet's *Parish Life in Mediæval England*)

There the members met to transact their business, and there they met for their dinners and amusements. It was a kind of parish club. Dr. Jessop wrote that "this church house or gild hall grew up as an institution which had become necessary when the social life of the parish had outgrown the accommodation which the church could afford, and when, indeed, there was just a trifle too much boisterous merriment and too little seriousness and sobriety to allow of the assemblies being held in the church at all. It became, in many places, one of the most important buildings in a parish."

It was a large building with a loft in which could be stored wood, lime, timber, sand, etc., and was often let to pedlars, or wandering merchants, to deposit their goods during the fair. There was a long, low room with a large fireplace and hearth, around which a dozen or more could sit in comfort. In the centre of the room was a large oak table. This was the scene of some very festive gatherings. The church house survived the Reformation. There was one in my parish of Barkham in 1603 which, with some land, belonged to the rector. Aubrey thus describes the building:

> In every parish was a church house, to which belonged spits, crocks, and other utensils for dressing provisions. Here the housekeepers met. The young people were there too, and had dancing, bowling, shooting at butts, etc., the ancients (*i.e.*, the old folks) sitting gravely by and looking on.

Here took place the " church ales," a very famous rural feast. The churchwardens bought and received presents of malt and hops, which they brewed into a light sweet beverage, and sold to the company. Other gifts would be received, perhaps a sheep, or a calf, and sometimes " geese and pyg and hare," and chickens and butter and eggs and spices were either bought or presented. Here, then, was a mighty spread, and dishes dainty enough "to set before the King." And right heartily did the rustics enjoy themselves, knowing that it was all in a good cause, and that the funds of the guild or the parish would benefit, especially as a collection was made during the banquet. In one instance, at Shire, Surrey, after paying all expenses, 38s. 7d. was left for the good of the parish, a sum equivalent in the present day, or, rather, pre-war days, to about £26. At Bramley the festivities lasted from Whit-Sunday to the following Wednesday (inclusive), not to mention a supper on the following Trinity Sunday. These feasts were often held four times a year, or as often as money was required. An arbour of boughs was erected in the churchyard, where the maidens collected money for the "ales." In later times these rural festivals degenerated, and the Puritans looked askance at them, and they were altogether prohibited.

There was a large amount of gaiety in the villages in those days. We often talk of trying in these days to enliven village life, and make men and women and children happier. Life is dull enough in some villages nowadays, and Dr. Jessop tells of the weariness of some young men in Cambridgeshire, whose only relaxation was a dreary walk along a dull flat road. They managed things better in mediæval times. There were many holidays in the course of the year, and what with May Day festivities, Plough Mondays, Hocktide and Shrovetide

MAY-DAY DANCERS: WINDOW, BETLEY HALL, STAFFS (TEMP. EDWARD IV.)

(From Cox's *Churchwardens' Accounts*)

sports, harvest suppers, fairs and "ales," the villagers had plenty of amusement.[1]

Municipal trading is not regarded in these days with much favour, and is not generally profitable. But in the fifteenth century it was carried on in villages for the good of the parish. The church-wardens did not confine their brewing to the church ales alone; they brewed at other times for any who wanted their beer, and the price of it went to fill the church chest. Bread was baked upon the same principle. To add to the enjoyment of their "ales," one or more minstrels were engaged. Sometimes, too, the villagers would act a miracle play, very badly perhaps, as we should think; and we might consider the scenes very rude, and perhaps blasphemous; but the acting of "Noah and his Sons" or the Nativity Play taught them many lessons about God and the Scriptures, besides adding much interest to their lives.

Almost every village seems to have had its company of players who visited the neighbouring towns and gave their performances. In the municipal accounts of Reading we find money and refreshments given, *lusoribus de Yatele* (Yateley), 3s. 4d.; and for the clothing of the minstrels, 5s. in 1419. In 1382 and 1388 to the players of Althermanstone (Aldermaston), 18d.; to the players of Wokingham, 2s. Twenty-seven adjacent villages contributed to the Bassingbourne Play in 1511. Plays were acted either in the church, or churchyard, or field nigh

[1] Some of these festivities I have described in my book on *Old English Customs*.

the church. At Harding, Norfolk, in 1452, payment was made for the original of an Interlude, for bread and ale to the Garblesham game. At Ashburton, Devon, for profit of ale, called players' ale, 32s. 4d.; also for players' clothing, for painting cloth for the players, and making tunics for pleirs (players) of Christmas game that playe in church, 2s.; for a "hed of here" (a head of hair—*i.e.*, a wig). Silk garment for Herod on Corpus Christi Day. Two devils' heads. Paye for gloves "for hym that played God Almighty." There was usually a feast after the play, when half a sheep, spices, bread, malt, etc., were consumed. At Bungay there was given to Kelsage the fool ("vyll") for his pastime before the play, 2s. Robin Hood with Maid Marian, and the whole joyous fellowship of Sherwood Forest used to take part in the summer plays. The villagers had companies of Robin Hood players, as Finchampstead had. They performed in Reading, and the churchwardens provided the clothes, a coat for Robin, five ells of canvas for "Made Maryon," a summer pole, breakfast, shoes for the Morris dancers, etc., and Robin and his merry men collected money from the crowd, called "Roben Hode money," gathering as much as 40s. 4d. at Croscombe, Somerset.

May Day and Whitsuntide brought special diversions, when there was much minstrelsy and music, and dancing of various sorts—such as Morris, Maypole, and hobby horse. At Tavistock in 1464 iid. was paid "To Mayers child for dawnsyng with the hobye hors." All over the country the same joyous meetings were held, and many pages could be filled with accounts of the same; but perhaps these recorded may be sufficient to show the extraordinary activity that existed, both in towns and villages, the diversity of amusements that brightened the lives of the rustics, and the great part that the church officials played in arranging these plays and feasts and merry diversions.

In the days before railways many of our villagers never strayed away far from their homes, and were very ignorant of the outside world. In mediæval times there were few who had not at some period of their lives gone on pilgrimage, and wandered away to the shrine of St. Thomas of Canterbury, or to Walsingham, or to Holywell, blessed by St. Winifred, in order to be cured of some disease or to fulfil a vow. Visits to markets in the towns, and to distant fairs, such as Stourbridge, near Cambridge, diversified their lives, and helped to make them contented. When they returned home and had fulfilled the vow they made when they scratched their votive cross on the arch of the church door, they would have much to tell of their adventures, of the remarkable characters they had met on the road. They had seen the King, bishops, abbots, monks and friars, pilgrims and beggars, jugglers and minstrels. They had lodged in the guest-house of a monastery, talked with solitary hermits by the wayside, and made acquaintance with all that strange weird world that lay outside their own beloved village. However, great changes were in store for that village, and for England, and the consideration of these must be deferred until the next chapter.

CHAPTER XIII

THE REFORMATION PERIOD

Changes at the Reformation—Dissolution of monasteries—Insurrections—New landowners—Sheep-farming—Ket's rebellion—Diminished power of the clergy—Church spoliation—Misery of the poor—New service-books—Mary's reign.

THE sixteenth century sun rose fair and smiling upon a happy England, but dark days were in store for the country. Strange stories reached the villages of Henry's tyranny, of the execution of many great men, of Wolsey's fall, and of the rise of a wretch named Cromwell, who advised the King to commit every enormity and wickedness. They heard that the Pope's rule over England was over, and were not sorry that they had to pay no more Peter's pence. And then they learnt of the fall of the monasteries, with all the turmoil and confusion that their suppression involved. The monks were great landowners, and the abbot and convent were lords of the manors of many a fair village. The Church, by its monasteries, controlled a large part of the countryside, and its influence extended far and wide. It is beyond the purpose of this book to tell the story of these religious houses, and the great work they accomplished in promoting the glory of God, in carrying on the great idea of continual worship in the noble buildings they erected, the cultivation of learning, both secular and religious, the education of youths in their schools, and the duty of extending hospitality to all classes. The monks were the pioneers in bringing into cultivation waste lands, and were the leaders in scientific farming and horticulture, and they taught the landowners many lessons in the useful art of the management of land. They utilised streams for water-power, for irrigation and sanitation; they sought out pure water for domestic use, and brought it long distances by conduits. The monks were liberal landlords, looked after their estates well, and after the welfare of their tenants and peasants. Not a few of their tenants, seated generation after generation on the monastic manors, grew into knightly or noble families. The monasteries also owned the advowson of very many parishes, and nominated the vicars who were to teach and minister to the people.

Hence it is evident that the monks exercised a very powerful influence throughout the land. Moreover, they were not unpopular. The powerful laymen were on good terms with them, and farmers and peasants liked and respected them. It is true that religious fervour had deserted the cloisters. The ranks of the religious had been terribly thinned by the Black Death, and many houses had never regained their full number of monks. The scandalous tales which the royal commissioners spread about their moral character were not credited by the people, and were mostly untrue. The King's agents reported, when the fate of the smaller monasteries was decided upon, that there were grievous scandals and abuses, and advised that the monks from these lesser houses should be transferred to " the great solemn monasteries of this realm, wherein—thanks be to God—religion is right well kept and observed." This testimony served not to save the greater houses when the unscrupulous King coveted their wealth and rich possessions.

That they were not unpopular is shown by the fact that the Act of Suppression was resisted in Parliament and only carried by the enforcement of the King's will and of his jackal, Cromwell. Moreover, the people rebelled and insurrections broke out in various parts of the country. In the North the Pilgrimage of Grace was a formidable but ill-led effort roused by the dissolution of the monasteries. The whole nobility of the northern counties with thirty thousand men rose in open revolt, and were conquered by guile and false promises, rather than by force of arms. Ruthless murder by hanging or the block followed, and many noble heads fell.

So the monasteries ceased, and their estates, which covered one-fifteenth of the whole of England, passed into the hands of the greedy King, who sold or gave them to his courtiers and friends. These men showed themselves indifferent landowners, caring only for their gains, and not for the comfort and welfare of their tenants. The monks were, doubtless, very easy-going as landlords and the monastic doles may have been somewhat demoralising; but their rule was far better than that of these absentee courtiers, who cared only for the lining of their purses by their merciless extortions. It is difficult to estimate the number of monks and nuns and friars and their dependants who were forced to leave the religious houses, and turned upon the world to shift for themselves and swell the pauper population of England. And this number was vastly increased by a process that was going on throughout the country. I have already stated that sheep-farming had become very profitable, owing to the need of wool, the great demand for it in foreign markets, and the prosperity of the cloth trade. The lords of the manor and the well-to-do farmers realised the advantages of keeping large flocks. These required less labour than ordinary agriculture. Hence their great policy was to get rid of their labourers, pull down their cottages, and turn the country into one vast sheep farm. In the later part of the reign of the first Tudor monarch, Henry VII., this evil had begun, and an Act was passed to check the evils arising from the decay of tillage and the destruction of villages. But very little improvement was wrought, and in 1514 Parliament again passed a legislative Act against engrossing farms—*i.e.*, doing away with small ones and throwing them into large ones, and ordering landlords to rebuild the houses that had been destroyed and to grow corn, instead of putting their land into pasture for sheep.

The wording of an Act passed ten years later clearly discloses the evils that had arisen. It states that rich men had devastated the land so much by sheep-farming that a marvellous number of people of this realm be not able to provide for themselves, their wives, and children, but be so discouraged with misery and poverty that they fall daily to theft and robbery, or pitifully die for hunger and cold." This statute fell on unwilling ears, and every imaginable device was resorted to to evade the law. As in these days, so then, when the Parliament was in difficulties, it appointed a commission to inquire into the matter. But there was the usual delay, the country was impatient, and rebellions arose. The most formidable rising took place in Norfolk under the leadership of Robert Ket, which was eventually crushed.

The dream of a "Merrie England" had quickly passed away from our rural villages. In the last century all had been going well, and the country was prosperous, and the prospect was fair. Freedom had arisen with all its blessings in its train, and now all the pleasant vision had vanished. Alien lords ruled over the broad acres of grass-lands, who were like greedy cormorants, and exacted every farthing they could get from the soil. Ruined homesteads, once happy homes, lined the village street bereft of thatch. The rector remained to care for his diminished flock, but he had seen many of his clerical neighbours seized by the spies of Cromwell and clapped into prison, and he dared not call his soul his own. These new lords, these *nouveaux riches,* were pestilential fellows who cared not for church or parson, and scrupled not to insult or quarrel with him. And in addition to the misfortunes of the village the commissioners of the King had visited the place, made an inventory of all the goods and beautiful ornaments and treasures of his church, and carried them off to swell the hideous heap of spoil in the royal exchequer. No wonder that the poor parson thought that the world was coming to an end. Especially did he regret that beautiful cope of blue velvet, which he delighted to wear when he marched in procession round the church, and that handsome silver-gilt chalice with which he celebrated the holy mysteries. Where was his silver pyx, and that vestment of damask red with flowers, his sweet-toned sanctus bell, and all the other things he loved so much? Not content with their spoil, the absence of which made his church look so bare and miserable, the greedy commissioners had broken into the chest of the guilds, and carried off much money, and had, by a royal edict, dissolved the Guild of St. Mary and the Ploughmen's Brotherhood and other fraternities. The sheep and cows belonging to these guilds they had driven away and sold, and even taken the honey and wax from the hives. No wonder the poor rector fell on his knees before his dismantled altar and wept bitterly, while his people could scarcely be restrained from throwing themselves upon the wretches who had plundered their church, and their guild, whereby their poor had been supported and their old folks helped.

The young King Edward was in the hands of an unscrupulous oligarchy who well-nigh ruined England. In spite of this robbery of church goods, of the destruction of the religious houses, chantries, and hospitals, and the spoliation of episcopal incomes and much else, he was heavily in debt, and all the wealth so iniquitously acquired had passed into the hands of his greedy courtiers. And everywhere there was misery in the dwellings of the poor, many of whom became vagrants and sturdy beggars, who thought little of robbing a traveller or pillaging a farmhouse.

I will not attempt to follow the changes that took place, the introduction of the new service-book which sounded somewhat strange to them when the rector said the words in English instead of the old Latin prayers and Psalms. Many resented the change, and there were riots in Devonshire, where the people cried again for the old Mass-book. But others were well content, and were glad to hear the English prayers and the reading of Holy Scripture in their own tongue, instead of in the Latin which they did not understand, and which had been a terrible incubus. And when their old parson died and a new rector came they were astonished at his ignorance, and also to find that he brought a wife with him, which rather offended their notions. Moreover, he was very poor, as his rich patron had made him give up to him most of the income of the living, leaving only a small pittance for himself. During that miserable reign of Edward VI., the affairs of the village and of the whole country were as bad as they could be. It was a time of terrible confusion, and of the unsettling of minds. Old Latimer said: "Never was there so much adultery, and so much divorcing." A sad picture the old divines draw of the state of England.

The churchwardens' accounts tell the story of the times, the destruction of rood-screens, the purloining of plate, and plundering of churches. At Ashburton, Devon, we find the entry: 1547. For taking down the rood and other images, 3s. 4d. 1549. For taking down the image and the tabernacles, and burning the same, 3s. 4d. In Mary's reign the rood was again set up, only to be taken down again when Elizabeth ruled. New books had to be purchased. In 1544 6d. was paid at Worksop for making four books in English for the "processions" —*i.e.*, for the Litany, which was sung in procession. The first Prayer-Book of Edward VI. was issued in 1549, and two years before this the "Order of Communion" was published. So the churchwardens of Melton Mowbray proceeded in that year to buy for 6s. a book off the nue service, and for 12d. "a saltre in ynglishe." The spelling in those days was a little curious, and the word Psalter caused much trouble to the scribes. We find it spelt Saulter, Salter, Saltre, etc. Other books were introduced into churches and chained, lest they should be carried away by too eager students. Some of these books were Bishop Hall's Sermons, *Foxe's Book of Martyrs*, the Paraphrases of Erasmus, Omelies (homilies) book, as well as the Holy Scriptures called "Bybyll," and many others of earlier or later times.

The people were not displeased when Mary came

to the throne. They were a little alarmed when they heard that she wished to restore the authority of the Pope; but his power had never been much felt in England as far as they remembered, and anything was better than Protector Somerset and his crew; and if the Queen wished to have the Pope, by all means let her do so, provided that Henry's daughter was as strong as her father, and gave them fair and just rule, and quietude and peace. They did not foresee the miserable fanaticism of the wretched woman egged on by her hateful Spanish husband; and when the shrieks and cries of the unhappy victims of her madness echoed through the land, they loathed and detested her, and longed for better days. Happily, they had not long to wait. Five years passed, and then her sister ruled, who again brought prosperity to the countryside, and cheered the hearts of her people.

CHAPTER XIV

THE ELIZABETHAN VILLAGE

Revival of agriculture—"Back to the land"—Harrison's *Description of England*—"New Gentlemen"—Rise of the yeomen—Improvement in farming—Hop-growing—The results of prosperity—English gardens—New buildings—Destruction of forests—The Elizabethan farmer—Fairs—Markets—Evils of purveyors—Shepherds—Milkmaids—Increased poverty—Rogues and vagabonds—Land-grabbers—Sports and games—"Merrie England."

THE farmers, clothiers, and woolmen of the Tudor period used to say:

> I thank my God and ever shal
> It was the sheep that payed for al.

In the last chapter we left them very busy with their useful fleeces, which brought much wealth into England and lined the pockets of the merchants and agriculturists. All the land was given up to grazing, and the farmers cared not for ploughing and sowing when they found that keeping sheep was more profitable. But in Queen Elizabeth's time rural affairs were altered. English wool declined in price, as it did in quality. Wheat rose in value from 6s. a quarter in Henry VIII.'s time to 36s. in the later years of Elizabeth. We have seen the distress that existed in the villages, and how, owing to the fact that sheep-farming required little labour, the peasants were driven out of their holdings, and had flocked to the towns, while their cottages were pulled down.

Now the cry, "back to the land," was raised. The men were called back to the country; cottages had to be built for them, and landlords and farmers, copyholders and labourers, shared in the increased prosperity of the countryside.

A valuable book by the Rev. William Harrison, entitled *A Description of England* (1577), throws much light upon the condition of the country in this period. He was rector of Radwinter and canon of Windsor. It is priceless to all students of Elizabethan times. One of the notable features of Elizabethan times was the rise of a new class of squires.

The old feudalism was dead, and Harrison wrote scornfully of their "new gentlemen." The rising generation of county magnates consisted of court favourites, who had contrived to ingratiate themselves with the Queen or her powerful ministers of State, and obtained grants of land or tithe, a dissolved abbey, or some other spoil of blood or sacrilege, for which they had watched patiently as a dog watches for a tossed bone; and mingled with this crowd of mercenary rascals were lawyers, monopolists, and usurers. Harrison states that anyone who studied the laws of the realm, abiding in the University, giving his mind to his books, or professed physic and liberal sciences, or became a captain in the wars, or benefited the commonwealth by good counsel given at home, living without manual labour, and able to bear the charges of a gentleman, could for money have a coat of arms bestowed upon him by heralds (who, in their charter, did of custom pretend antiquity and service and many gay things, and thus make good profit) —anyone so distinguished could be called " master," the title of esquire, and gentleman, and be reputed a gentleman ever after. It is all of no consequence, Harrison concludes. The Sovereign loses nothing. If " the gentleman " be called to the wars he pays for his own outfit. His title hurts no one but himself, who perhaps will go in wider breeches than his legs will bear, or as the proverb says: " Now and then bear a bigger sail than his boat is able to carry."

The rise of the yeoman in social importance was a feature of the country life of this period, a noble class of men, the backbone of England, who, as Harrison says, in time past made all France afraid, and they were, and are, respected in their neighbourhood, though agricultural depression has in modern days almost deprived them of their lands. They were farmers of their own holdings, and in Elizabethan times they throve and increased their gains. They often farmed, also, the squire's lands, grazed cattle, frequented the markets, kept servants, were shrewd and clever, and became rich. They often bought up the properties of poor and unthrifty gentlemen, sent their sons to the University and the Inns of Court, and made them gentlemen.

Sir Thomas Overbury in his *Characters*, pub-

View of Great Tew, Oxfordshire

lished in 1614-15, gives us an amusing and graphic description of the yeoman:

His outside is an ancient yeoman of England, though his inside may give arms (with the best gentlemen) and ne'er see the herald. There is no truer servant in the house than himself. Though he be master, he says not to his servants, "Go to field," but "Let us go"; and with his own eye doth both fatten his flock, and set forward all manner of husbandry. He is taught by nature to be contented with a little; his own fold yields him both food and raiment: he is pleased with any nourishment God sends, whilst curious gluttony ransacks, as it were, Noah's Ark for food, only to feed the riot of one meal. He is ne'er known to go to law; understanding, to be law-bound among men, is like to be hide-bound among his beasts; they thrive not under it: and that such men sleep as unquietly, as if their pillows were stuffed with lawyers' penknives. When he builds, no poor tenant's cottage hinders his prospect: they are indeed his almshouses, though there be painted on them no such superscription. He never sits up late, but when he hunts the badger, the vowed foe of his lambs: nor uses he any cruelty, but when he hunts the hare; nor subtlety, but when he setteth snares for the snipe, or pitfalls for the blackbird; nor oppression, but when in the month of July, he goes to the next river, and shears his sheep. He allows of honest pastime, and thinks not the bones of the dead any thing bruised, or the worse for it, though the country lasses dance in the churchyard after evensong. Rock Monday, and the wake in summer, shrovings, the wakeful ketches on Christmas Eve, the hockey or seed cake, these he yearly keeps, yet holds them no relics of popery.[1] He is not so inquisitive after news derived from the privy closet, when the finding an aerie of hawks in his own ground, or the foaling of a colt come of a good strain are tidings more pleasant, more profitable. He is

[1] *I.e.*, as the Puritans did.

lord paramount within himself, though he hold by never so mean a tenure; and dies the more contentedly (though he leave his heir young) in regard he leaves him not liable to a covetous guardian. Lastly, to end him; he cares not when his end comes, he needs not fear his audit, for his quietus is in heaven.

Harrison tells us that the soil of England is very fruitful, but better for grazing than for tilling. Three-fourths of the country was pasture and one-fourth arable. Good farming had made the land more fruitful than of yore, and the farmers used plenty of dung and white marl, which was better than chalk, and had become more " painful "—*i.e.*, painstaking—skilful, and careful than they used to be. They reaped better harvests in small acreage than in much larger space, owing to their previous idleness and negligent ways. The greatest improvement was in Wales, where in former days the folk were idle and dissolute, and spent their time in picking and stealing from each other; whence arose the rhyme about " Taffy was a Welshman, Taffy was a thief: Taffy came to my house, and stole a piece of beef," etc. The pasture was mostly fine and rich, so much so that the cattle were speedily fatted, or yielded a great abundance of milk and cream, which provided the yellowest butter and the finest cheese. Wales had the best pasture land, and the county of Cardigan was as fertile as Italy, which, in the learned author's opinion, was deemed the Paradise of the World, but on account of the wickedness of the inhabitants he declared it to be the " very sink and drain of Hell."

Hop-growing had been introduced in moory and unprofitable lands, which were thus made to yield such increase that few farmers had not hop-gardens; and the hops produced were far better than those imported from Flanders. By twelve acres of hops a man could clear 200 marks (£133 6s. 8d.). English cattle were far better than those of any other country. The oxen were larger, taller, and heavier. The sheep provided better meat, and finer fleece, and were more prolific than any abroad; and so did the goats surpass any others. But England, he regrets, produced no wine, owing to the negligence of his countrymen; although in former times they did so, as he discovered by his researches. There used to be tithes on wine, and abbey vineyards. The Isle of Ely was called the Isle of Vines. It was no fault of the soil, but national idleness, that caused the decay of the industry.

Some of the characteristics which Harrison found blameworthy are not wanting in our own time. He found that trade with foreign countries made our people rich, and consequently idle. They left off their former industrious ways and frugal living, and gave themselves to excess and vanity. Hence our country failed to produce things; and foreigners, perceiving our sluggishness and idleness, sent us supplies from abroad. This tended to increase our idleness. When you can get things at a reasonable cost from abroad, why spend time and trouble in producing the same at home? Thus the people said, and thus they became enemies to their own welfare. They imagined that foreign goods were superior to those produced at home. Harrison agrees with our modern statesmen, and urges his countrymen to produce more and work harder. The modern political economist will cordially agree with him, when he says that "the maintenance of a superfluous number of dealers in most trades (tillage always excepted) is one of the greatest causes why prices of things become excessive." Evidently middlemen were not more in favour three centuries ago than they are to-day.

In the sixteenth century and after, the gardens of England had attained to a high degree of beauty. The gardens of the Hesperides were not equal to ours. Harrison tells of his own little garden, only three hundred square feet in size, but containing no less than three hundred simples of rare quality, and difficult to be procured, and concludes: "If, therefore, my own little plot, void of all cost in keeping, be so well furnished, what shall we think of those of Hampton Court, Nonsuch, Theobalds, Cobham Garden, and sundry others appertaining to divers citizens of London? He laments over the destruction of our forests, and therein, too, we have cause to agree with him. The Elizabethans were always building, and used nothing but oak for their timber houses. They had used as much oak in ten years as their sires had done in a hundred. There was a vast amount of building going on. Amateur architects were always imagining new devices, setting up and pulling down, enlarging their houses or contracting them, whereby "their heads are never idle, their purses never shut, or their books of accounts never made perfect." Harrison did not approve of the new fashion of building many chimneys. In spite of them his compatriot tenderlings constantly complained of rheumatism, catarrhs, and colds. When they had only reredoses in their halls, they did not suffer from headaches. The smoke hardened the timbers, and also the men, keeping away colds and other ills.

So the trees were felled, and the forests disappeared. Timber was wanted for the navy. The smelting of iron in Kent and Sussex consumed much wood, and landowners and farmers grubbed up woods to convert the land into sheep-walks, all of which our author considered to be detrimental to the country, and harmful to the nation—a word of caution that is needed at the present time when the necessities of war-time have denuded our country of so much timber and laid low our woods.

And here I may recall the description of an Elizabethan farmer, as he is depicted by a contemporary writer, John Stephens, in his work entitled, *Essays and Characters*, published in 1615. It is at once graphic and amusing:

> A farmer is a concealed commodity. His worth or value is not fully known till he be half rotten: and then he is worth nothing. He hath religion enough to say, God bless his Majesty; God send peace, and fair weather: so that one may glean harvest out of him to be his time of happiness: but the tithe-sheaf goes against his conscience; for he had rather spend the value upon his reapers and ploughmen than bestow any thing to the maintenance of a parson. He is sufficiently book-read, nay a profound

doctor, if he can search into the diseases of cattle: and to foretell rain by tokens makes him a miraculous astronomer. To speak good English is more than he much regards; and for him not to contemn all arts and languages, were to condemn his own education. The pride of his housekeeping is a mess of cream, a pig, or a green goose; and if his servants can uncontrolled find the highway to the cupboard, it wins the name of a bountiful yeoman. Doubtless he would murmur against the Tribune's law, by which none might occupy more than five hundred acres, for he murmurs against himself, because he cannot purchase more. To purchase arms (if he emulates gentry) sets upon him like an ague: it breaks his sleep, takes away his stomach, and he can never be quiet till the herald hath given him the harrows, the cuckoo, or some ridiculous emblem for his armoury. The bringing up and marriage of his eldest son is an ambition which afflicts him so soon as the boy is born, and the hope to see his son superior, or placed above him, drives him to dote upon the boy in his cradle. To peruse the statutes, and prefer them before the Bible makes him purchase the credit of a shrewd fellow; and then he brings all adversaries to composition; and if at length he can discover himself in large legacies beyond expectation, he hath his desire. Meantime, he makes the prevention of a dearth his title to be thought a good commonwealth's man. And therefore he preserves a chandler's treasure of bacon, links and puddings in the chimney corner. He is quickly and contentedly put into the fashion, if his clothes be made against Whitsuntide, or Christmas day: and then outwardly he contemns appearance. He cannot therefore choose but hate a Spaniard likewise, and (he thinks) that hatred only makes him a loyal subject: for benevolence and subsidies be more unseasonable to him, than his quarter's rent. Briefly, being a good housekeeper, he is an honest man and so, he thinks of no rising higher, but rising early in the morning; and being up, he hath no end of motion, but wanders in his woods and pastures so continually, that when he sleeps, or sits, he wanders also. After this, he turns into his element, by being too venturous hot, and cold: then he is fit for nothing but a chequered grave: howsoever some may think him convenient to make an everlasting bridge; because his best foundation has been (perhaps) upon wool-packs.

Trade was carried on in fairs and markets. We had in England such gigantic fairs as Stourbridge, near Cambridge, and Bartholomew Fair at Smithfield; and every town and some villages had fairs, which were bestowed upon them by royal grants. Fairs are of ecclesiastical origin, as their name denotes. Fair is the Latin *feria* or holy day, and it would be interesting to show how in the East the great gatherings for religious observances became the centres of organised trading; such as the great fair held in the eleventh century on Mount Calvary, on September 15 every year, where the productions of Europe were exchanged for those of the East. The German name *messen,* derived from the Mass or feast, seems also to denote the ecclesiastical origin of fairs. Weekly markets were held in most towns for the convenience of buyers, to which agricultural produce was brought for sale. There seem to have been many tricks in the trade. The inspection of the goods was imperfectly carried out, and if a country baker brought to the market good bread, fault was found with it by the townsfolk who wanted to sell their own bread, and he was obliged to return home with his goods unsold. Moreover, there was much drunkenness at these gatherings, caused by "heady ale and beer, called by people hussecap, mad dog, angels' food, and dragon's milk." Malt bugs hugged at ale-pots like pigs at their dame's teats, till they were as red as cocks, and little wiser than their combs.

Bodgers and loaders and common carriers bought up all the corn, and then raised the price, so that the poor man could not purchase his weekly stock. Much corn was exported to the detriment of the home consumer. The bodgers were terrible folk, and were guilty of all manner of deceit. They kept the corn to enhance the price until it was musty, and then the poor were forced to buy it, and it gave them the plague. The royal purveyors caused much hardship to the farmers. They had the right of buying goods for the Sovereign's use at less than market price. They bought all kinds of farm produce—butter, cheese, pigs, capons, hens, hogs, and bacon—and then permitted their wives to sell these goods elsewhere, raising the prices, and profiting by the transaction. There were too many dealers. There were no standard weights and measures, and these wretched dealers bought by one measure, the larger one, and sold by a smaller one. These and other tricks were resorted to by these infamous creatures, who cheated the poor and wronged the nation. However, in spite of abuses the markets were useful institutions. They supplied the neighbourhood with all that the people required, and there was scarcely a town throughout the country which had not its weekly market, and once or twice a year its fair.

Of the labouring rustic we have a few glimpses in the writings of contemporary scribes. Shakespeare has given us in *As You Like It* a description of a shepherd. Corin says:

Sir, I am a true labourer: I earn that I eat, get that I wear, owe no man hate, envy no man's happiness, glad of other men's good, content with my harm; and the greatest of my pride is to see my ewes graze and my lambs suck.

Another writer, John Stephens, in *Essays and Characters* (1615), gives another picture of this worthy:

An honest shepherd is a man that well verifies the Latin piece, *qui bene latuit bene vixit:* he lives well that lives retired: for he is always thought the most innocent because he is least public: and certainly I cannot well resolve you whether his sheep or he be more innocent. Give him fat lambs and fair weather, and he knows no happiness beyond them. He shows, most fitly among all professions, that nature is contented with a little. For the sweet fountain is his fairest alehouse: the sunny bank his best chamber. Adam had never less need of neighbours' friendship; nor was at any time troubled with neighbours' envy less than he: the next grove or thicket will defend him from a shower: and if they be not so favourable, his homely palace is not far distant. He proves quietness to be best contentment, and that there is no quietness like a certain rest. His flock affords him his whole raiment, outside and linings, cloth and leather; and instead of much costly linen, his little garden yields hemp enough to make his lockram shirts: which do preserve his body sweetened against court-itch and poxes, as a sear-cloth sweetens carcasses. He gives the just epitome of a contented man: for he is neither daunted with lightning and thunder, nor overjoyed with springtime and harvest. His daily life is a delightful work, whatsoever the work be; whether to mend his garments, cure a diseased sheep, instruct his dog, or change pastures: and these be pleasant actions, because voluntary, patient, not interrupted. He comprehends the true pattern of a moderate wise man: for as a shepherd, so a moderate man hath the supremacy over his thoughts and passions: neither hath he any affection of so wild a nature, but he can bring it into good order, with an easy whistle. The worst temptation of his idleness teaches him no further mischief, than to love entirely some nut-brown milkmaid, or hunt the squirrel, or make his cosset wanton. He may turn many rare esteemed physicians into shame and blushing: for whereas they, with infinite compounds and fair promises, do carry men to death the furthest way about; he with a few simples preserves himself and family to the most lengthened sufferance of nature. Tar and honey be his mithridates and syrups; the which, together with a Christmas carol, defend his desolate life from cares and melancholy. With little knowledge and a simple faith, he purifies his honest soul, in the same manner as he can wash his body in an obscure fountain, better than in the wide ocean. When he seems lazy and void of action, I dare approve his harmless negligence, rather than many approved men's diligence. Briefly he is the perfect allegory of a most blessed governor: and he that will pursue the trope's invention, may make this character a volume

A companion portrait is that of

> A fair and happy milkmaid,
> The queen of curds and cream.

as Shakespeare dubs her in *The Winter's Tale,* such a one as the Princess Elizabeth saw and envied in the park at Woodstock, "singing pleasantlie," while she herself was a close prisoner. This is the portrait that Sir Thomas Overbury painted:

A fair and happy milkmaid is a country wench, that is so far from making herself beautiful by art, that one look of hers is able to put all face-physic out of countenance. She knows a fair look is but a dumb orator to commend virtue, therefore minds it not. All her excellencies stand in her so silently, as if they had stolen upon her without her knowledge. The lining of her apparel (which is herself) is far better than outsides of tissue: for though she be not arrayed in the spoil of the silkworm, she is decked in innocency, a far better wearing. She doth not, with lying long abed, spoil both her complexion and conditions. Nature hath taught her too immoderate sleep is rust to the soul. She rises therefore with chanticleer, her dame's cock, and at night makes the lamb her curfew. In milking a cow, and straining the teats through her fingers, it seems that so sweet a milk-press makes the milk the whiter or sweeter; for never came almond glove or aromatic ointment on her palm to taint it. The golden ears of corn fall and kiss her feet when she reaps them, as if they wished to be bound and led prisoners by the same hand that felled them. Her breath is her own, which scents all the year long of June, like a new-made hay-cock. She makes her hand hard with labour, and her heart soft with pity: and when winter evenings fall early (sitting at her merry wheel) she sings a defiance to the giddy wheel of fortune. She doth all things with so sweet a grace, it seems ignorance will not suffer her to do ill, being her mind is to do well. She bestows her year's wages at next fair; and in choosing her garments, counts no bravery in the world like decency. The garden and beehive are all her physic and chirurgery, and she lives the longer for it. She dares go alone and unfold sheep in the night, and fears no manner of ill, because she means none: yet to say truth, she is never alone, for she is still accompanied with old songs, honest thoughts and prayers, but short ones: yet they have their efficacy, in that they are not palled with ensuing idle cogitations. Lastly, her dreams are so chaste, that she dare tell them; only a Friday's dream is all her superstition: that she conceals for fear of anger. Thus lives she, and all her care is she may die in the springtime, to have store of flowers stuck upon her winding-sheet.

That is a very pretty picture, and we hope that she and Colin fell in love and made a match of it and lived happily ever afterwards.

In spite of the increased prosperity of the countryside, there was much poverty and distress in the land. Rogues and vagabonds had increased enormously and experienced hard times. This increase was due partly to the dissolution of the monasteries, but chiefly to economic reasons. As I have already stated, the progress of sheep-farming in the time of the early Tudors, and consequently the decrease in agricultural employment, had driven the labourers from the village into the towns, where work could not be found for them; and in spite of the call back to the land many had drifted into vagabondage and become sturdy and sometimes dangerous beggars. Modern experience has taught us that when a man becomes a tramp, it is very difficult to reclaim him and to get him to settle down to regular work. It was so in the sixteenth and seventeenth centuries. Harrison states that in his time (1566) there were no less than ten thousand tramps and rogues, who, following the example of the "Egyptians" or gipsies, had devised a language of their own called "canting," or "pedlar's French," composed partly of odd words of their own devising, which no one could understand but themselves. His estimate was too low. In 1569 a search was made, and no less than thirteen thousand were rounded up. The poor were divided into three classes: the impotent; those who had lost their work and made poor by accident; and the thriftless, who became rogues and vagabonds. For the first two classes, the true poor, whom Christ bids us feed, weekly collections were made throughout the land, and it was found necessary to establish by various Acts of Parliament—of which there were four passed in Elizabeth's reign—a system of poor relief. The only remedy they could devise to cure vagrants was to whip them in the towns through which they wandered.

In a previous book of mine I have referred to these methods of curing tramps. In the records of Hungerford there are several references to whipping tramps. The whip is still preserved, and it is not a very formidable implement. The lashes are very thin, and could not have hurt the victim very much. It must have been simple child's play when compared with an Eton birching. Moreover, the victims were given money, usually 2d., to help them on their way to the next town, where the process would be repeated.

Thus, at Melton Mowbray there is a record of the payments of 2d. to "Robert Moodee for wipping tow poore folkes," and 2d. "gave them when they were wipped."

The worthy Harrison has some very harsh words against the sin of covetous people who grabbed land, and turned men out of their holdings for their own gain. "At whose hand shall the blood of these men be required?" he asks in scorn. The dispossessed either emigrated or joined the ranks of the ever-increasing bands of wanderers. These beggars must have been a great nuisance, as they used to counterfeit sickness and make hideous sores upon their bodies, so as to excite the pity of the passers-by. Some were thieves, robbers, rufflers, and a host of others, whose names are a puzzle —*e.g.*, Palliards, Fraters, Abrahams, freshwater mariners, whipjacks, dummerers, and others, both male and female.

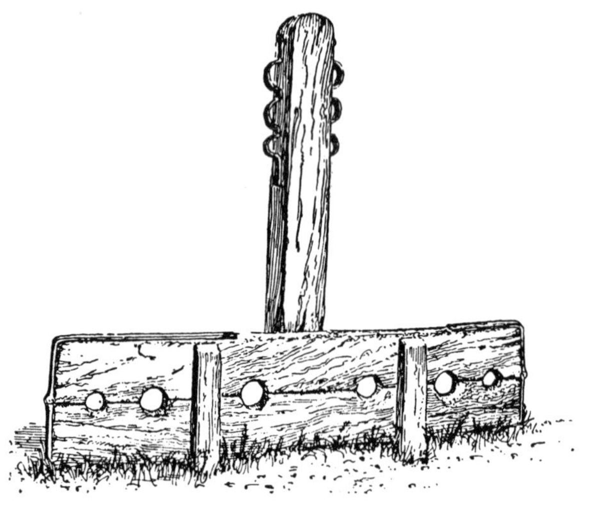

STOCKS AND WHIPPING-POST, UFFORD, SUFFOLK
(From Cox's *Churchwardens' Accounts*)

These were guilty of all kinds of crime, and various punishments were inflicted, whipping, burning through the ears with a third-inch hot iron, and, in case of contumacy, death. Amongst the tramps, who falsely pretended to be licensed to ply their calling, were cofiners, unlawful gamesters, physiognomists, palmists, fortune-tellers, fencers, players, minstrels, jugglers, pedlars, tinkers, pretended scholars at the Universities, shipmen and bearwards. These bear-leaders had been the cause of many children's deaths. Stocks and whipping-posts, ducking-stools and branks, were in constant use. These last were much in vogue for scolding women, terrible instruments of torture which poor women had to endure who had dared to protest

DUCKING-STOOL FOR A SCOLD (FROM AN OLD CHAP BOOK)

(From Cox's *Churchwardens' Accounts*)

against the vagaries of drunken or faithless husbands, or to speak their minds to a local tyrant dressed in the garb of a brief authority.

The unfortunate person who had to inflict parochial punishments was the constable, an important official, who was responsible for many matters. His was an ancient office, dating back fourteen centuries, and he had various names, such as tythingman, headborough, provost, and then constable. In villages he was known as petty-constable, and as we shall see presently he received at Barkham two guineas for his pains. His duty was also to see that his parish provided the prescribed armour, and the equipment of one or more soldiers whom each parish had to send to the national army. In the time of the Edwards one foot-soldier, fully armed and equipped for sixty days, had to be provided. In time of special need a larger number was required. In Elizabeth's time the constable had to provide at the expense of the parish a musket, an arquebuse or lighter gun, a flask for powder and bandolier, a pike, morion, or helmet, corslet of leather. This was stored in the room over the porch, commonly called a parvise. The constable had to see to the making and repair of the parish butts for archery practice, and the providing of bows of yew and arrows. And then, when bows became obsolete in warfare, the constable had to procure stores of gunpowder, bullets, and match. All these were stored within the churches, and it is wonderful that they were not all blown up. At Cheddar there is a charge of 12s. "for setting up a frame in the churche to hange the armor upon." There are countless references to these things in the old account books, but for these I have no space.

Hunting and hawking were the general sports of the gentry, and the villagers would often witness gay companies riding forth in pursuit of

> the timorous hare,
> Or at the fox which lives by subtlety,
> Or at the roe which no encounter dare.

They would watch the poor hare "outrunning the wind," "cranking and crossing with a thousand doubles," seeking refuge amongst a flock of sheep, or a herd of deer or rabbits, and then, far off upon a hill, "standing on hinder legs with listening ear":

> To hearken if his foe pursue him still:
> Anon their loud alarum he doth hear,
> And now his grief may be compared well
> To one sore sick that hears the passing bell.

The villagers used to practise archery, though it was dying out in the service of war. There were contests on village greens; and in Clewer Church, near Windsor, there is a brass to the memory of a redoubtable champion, Martin Expence, who, at Bray, "shott with 100 men him selfe alone." Football was a popular game, and it was of a very rough variety, with general hacking, tripping, and charging the opponents. No wonder James I. tried to abolish it, declaring it was "meeter for laming than making able the users thereof."

In my book on *The England of Shakespeare* I have told the story of a football match at North Moreton, in Berkshire, as revealed by an account of a terrible affair that happened in 1598. The entry in the register records the burial of two men, Richard and John Gregorie, and states: "These two men were killed by ould Gunter. Gunter's sonnes and the Gregories fell together by ye yeares [ears] at football. Ould Gunter drew his dagger and broke both their heads, and they died both within a fortnight after." Sad to relate, old

Gunter was the parson of the parish. Doubtless he was witnessing the savage game. His sons and the Gregories were playing fiercely in the scrum. He saw the boys overthrown by their opponents, and fearing for their lives and carried away by excitement, drew his dagger and struck the fatal blows. This is a curious revelation of the fierceness of Elizabethan football, which is borne out by many contemporary writers—Barclay, Waller, and Stubbes—whose evidence I have no space to quote.

Athletic contests were numerous, such as the Cotswold games at Dover's Hill, Chipping-Campden, which consisted of coursing matches, leaping, cudgel-playing, fighting with sword and buckler, pitching the bar, and tossing the pike. English folk have always loved dancing, and feet were as nimble on the village greens at this period as at any other time. On May Days and other rural festivals the lads and lassies tripped it merrily on the green-sward, until Puritans, like Philip Stubbes, tried to stop "the horrible vice of pestiferous dancing." He calls it "the noble science of heathen devilrie," and one that no Christian may indulge in. It was certainly a vigorous pastime, if he proclaims truly that "some have broke their legs with skipping, leaping, turning, and vawting, and some have come to one hurt, and some to another."

Sheep-shearing brought many joys. The festival is described in Shakespeare's *Winter's Tale*. There were many high days and holidays to be observed, especially Christmas, with its feasts and jollifications, when rich men kept open house and all poor labourers were invited. There were the diversions of Plough Monday, May Day, Eastertide, and Hocktide. Fires were lighted on St. John's Eve, and Harvest Homes were popular rejoicings. Hentzner fortunately witnessed a Harvest Home in Berkshire, and thus describes it:

> As we were returning to our inn, we happened to meet some country people celebrating their harvest-home: their last load of corn they crown with flowers, having besides an image richly dressed, by which, perhaps, they signify Ceres; this they keep moving about, while the men and women and men and maid servants, riding through the streets in the cart, shout as hard as they can till they arrive at the barn.

Such scenes as these, such boisterous jollities and good nature, such pastimes, games, and sports, helped to make England a "Merrie England," such as we have never really known since; and though times were often hard, and poor folks plentiful, and plagues frequent, and life uncertain, village life was happier then than at any other period, and the joy of life greater, in spite of the wailing of Master Stubbes and other Puritan declamations.

CHAPTER XV

THE STUART PERIOD

Agricultural prosperity—Appearance of the village—Old cottages—Manor-houses—Open-field cultivation—New landlords—Norden's *Surveyor's Dialogue*—Books on agriculture—The Flemings—Reclamation of the Fens—The Civil War—The Effects of Puritanism—The *Book of Sports*—Stubbes's *Anatomie of Abuses*—Sufferings of the clergy—The Restoration—Rise of the middle classes—The effects of the war—Abolition of purveyance—Improvement of agriculture—A squire's hospitality—Popularity of the Church.

AS we have seen in the last chapter, during the days of good Queen Bess much song and laughter echoed through the land, and "Merrie England"—a vain will-o'-the-wisp sort of expression applied by people to some former vague period of existence when everyone was happy and contented, and sin, poverty, and misery were things unknown—was then more or less realised, perhaps more than at any subsequent time in our history. Nor did the condition of the country change materially when the foolish "Solomon of the North," as James I. was ridiculously and satirically called, ascended the English throne. Agriculture continued to prosper. The price of corn had increased enormously, and was selling at £5 4s. a quarter,[1] and both landlords and farmers flourished.

[1] It is curious to note the fluctuations. In 1499 corn was 4s. a quarter; in 1521, 20s.; in 1550, 8s.; in 1574, £2 16s.

The village had begun to assume the appearance which most of us who live in old-fashioned English hamlets know so well, and in which we take so much delight. It forms a pretty picture—this village—which is in danger of being defaced. Around the village green are grouped several cottages with thatched roofs, high gables, and projecting barge-boards skilfully carved or pierced with tracery in the form of trefoils or quatrefoils. At this time the builders finished off the ends of the gables at the eaves with pendants, and adorned the ridge with a finial. There is a corner post formed of the butt of a tree placed root upwards, with the top part curving diagonally outwards in order to carry the angle-posts of the upper story. There are large upright timbers and horizontal beams which make squares of framework, and these are divided into smaller squares, which are filled, some with windows and the others with "wattle and daub." I could fill the rest of this book with descriptions of these old cottages. They are now threatened by these new housing schemes. Pray use your influence to prevent such a catastrophe. Improve them, enlarge them, and adapt them to modern needs, but do not let them be pulled down.

The squire, too, has been building for himself a new manor-house, and a very graceful one it is, standing in a sweet old-fashioned garden. It has a central hall with two wings, and a fine porch with a room over it, the plan forming the letter **E**; it was not fashioned as a compliment to Queen Elizabeth, though perhaps some courteous squire may have told her that such was the case. There are high twisted chimney-stacks, tall gables, red-tiled roofs, a gateway flanked by heavy buttresses, and an encircling wall with sunk bays, and much else that is delightful. The church retains externally its Norman characteristics, in spite of all the changes that the centuries have wrought. There is a village inn with a smithy next door to it, and the smith has fashioned some charming iron-work to support the sign-board, displaying a conventional "Bull." There are picturesque farm-houses surrounded by stacks of hay and corn, and the village is a hive of industry.

The open-field cultivation is continued by the peasant farmers, and enclosures are constantly being made. A new race of landowners has come into being. Agriculture, being prosperous, has attracted to the countryside the denizens of towns. Fynes Morison tells us that "lawyers, citizens, and vulgar men" have come into the country and acquired farms and manors, intent upon making fortunes. They were a sorry type, these new landlords, hard masters, rapacious and cruel. When a tenant's lease expired they would levy heavy exactions, raise the rent, offer the new lease to competition; and the tenant had to pay a high price for renewal, or give up the farm to another. This was exceptionally hard, as in former times sons succeeded fathers as tenants, and the land had been held by one family for many generations. Also, these new men exacted heavy fines on the copyholders, who thus became a prey to the rapacity of their landlords, and were squeezed out of the village. Neither was the old system of bond-service entirely eradicated. John Norden, in his *Surveyor's Dialogue* (1608), states that there were some without manumission, few known, but more concealed, although many lords had voluntarily released their tenants from such slavery. "Truly, I think it a Christian part so to do; for seeing we be now all as the children of one father, the servants of one God, and the subjects of one King, it is very uncharitable to retain our brethren in bondage: since, when we were all bond, Christ did make us free." Such is the admirable conclusion of the dialogue between the lord of the manor and the surveyor.

But these new men determined to get as much out of their land as possible, turned their attention to the improvement of agricultural methods. Several books on farming appeared, such as Hartlib's *Legacy of Husbandry*, Norden's *The Surveyor's Dialogue*, (1608), Blith's *English Improver Improved* (1652), Worledge's *Systema Agriculturæ*, Rowland Vaughan on *Irrigation* (1610), Markham's *The English Husbandman* (1613), and others. Great attention was paid to manuring. The introduction of the turnip, the potato, and clover, marked great progress, and paved the way to the revolutionising of farming. Under the old system each field lay fallow every third year. By growing green crops the whole land was kept under cultivation year after year. Livestock was improved in breed and condition; winter feeding came into use; fresh vegetables took root in the kitchen garden, and fresh fruit-trees in the orchard. Objection was taken to the planting of apples, pear-trees, and crab-stocks in hedges, between fields and orchards, lest the fruit should be stolen; but Norden's Surveyor states that in Kent, Shropshire, and other counties, this has been done with much profit, that a good mind will not grudge a wayfaring passenger an apple or a pear, and that the fruit crop will yield excellent cider and perry, enough to satisfy a whole household, and make an overplus of ten pounds more or less.

In our villages did the faces of the labourers show content? I trow not. They did not share much in the prosperity of the countryside. Although the prices were higher, the wages remained much the same as before, and their lives were harder. The standard of living in all classes had risen. The husbandman tried to live like the yeoman, the yeoman as the gentleman, the gentleman as the squire, and the squire as his superior. More than thirty times as much money was spent by a family as before. There was much frequenting of alehouses and taverns, and playing at dice and cards. People gave themselves too much to ease and pleasure, especially in the West Country, near Taunton, the Paradise of England.

The industrious Flemings helped greatly in English agriculture, and to them it owed the cultivation of turnips and grass seeds, and that important work, the reclamation of the Fens. The Romans had begun it, and the monks of Croyland, Ely, and other monasteries, had continued it, but it was left to the Earl of Bedford and his friends to attempt it on a large scale. It was an immense undertaking, and was only partially successful, being interrupted by the great call to arms in the Civil War.

It is impossible in this book to discuss the causes that led to this convulsion, though many were connected with country life. The old families naturally showed their traditional loyalty, and spent their blood and treasure for the King. The new men, "the lawyers, citizens, and vulgar men," about whom Fynes Morison wrote, liked not the relics of feudalism that lingered on, the Sovereign's rights about wardship, and the abuses of purveyance, of which I have spoken. James I. alienated his subjects by his weakness and meanness, exasperated Parliament, and left his son a legacy of troubles, which the cleverest statecraft would scarcely have been able to disperse. The ablest King could hardly have satisfied the nation, and Charles was not an able King. He tried to play the part of a powerful Tudor, revived obsolete taxes, such as ship money, and as a result the country was soon in a blaze, and the Civil War began, with what results we know full well. Hundreds of estates were confiscated, many landowners ruined, and in some parts of the country where the fighting was most fierce and frequent, as in Berkshire, farms and fertile fields were devastated. Companies of starved soldiery roved the country and plundered the farms, breaking and robbing houses, and driving off sheep and other cattle, and killing any who resisted them.

Both armies were obliged to pillage the country for supplies, and the poor farmers had little livestock left. In many other parts of the country the ploughing and sowing, reaping and mowing, went on as usual.

In many accounts we find charges for billeting soldiers, "lodging for the troophers," for dressing the church after the soldiers and for frankincense to sweeten it. The soldiers took 30s. out of the poor man's box, and stabling their horses in churches was a common practice.

Great changes were wrought in the social habits of the villagers by the Puritans. They were a bitter, narrow-souled crew, who saw only the dark side of everything, evil in innocence, sin in mirth, the devil in dancing, and hell in play-acting. It had been the custom of English folk after afternoon service on Sunday to enjoy archery, games, dancing, and other like amusements. Sometimes in towns the cruel sports of bear-baiting and bull-baiting were not unknown, but I doubt whether these were common practices in villages. In Elizabeth's time (1572) Thomas Cartwright began his invectives against Sunday games, and these flourished, especially in Lancashire, where the population was mainly Roman Catholic. The Puritans tried to stop these Sunday pastimes, but when James I. made his progress through the County Palatine, on hearing the complaints of the people he listened to their petition, and granted their request for permission to continue their Sunday sports. Then followed the issue of The King's *Book of Sports*, which, while prohibiting unlawful pastimes such as the baiting of beasts, permitted them to dance and

To throw the sledge,
To jump, or leap over ditch, or hedge;
To wrastle, play at stoole ball,[1] or to runne,
To pitch the barre or to shoot of a gunne,
To play at loggets, nine holes, or ten pinnes,
To trye it out at football by the shinnes.

The King approved of May-Day festivities, and fairs and wakes and holidays, all of which were gall and wormwood to the Puritans. Charles I. renewed the *Book of Sports*, and thereby aroused their anger. I should like to tell you what they said, but space forbids. You can read their fearful phillipics and condemnations in Stubbes's *Anatomie of Abuses* and other Puritan literature. Stubbes had excellent intentions, and much that he wrote was wise and good; but he and his fanatical brethren saw evil in that which was not evil, and condemned the innocent as well as the guilty. In the first year of Charles I. the Government, led by the Puritan faction, condemned all Sunday sports and the observance of Saints' Days as holidays. And so Merrie England was very sad. The minstrels sang no more, even the bells in the church tower were silent, except for service. No more dancing on the village green, no more sports and merry-makings. A blight fell on the spirits of young men and maidens. Church ales and Whitsuntide rejoicings ceased. Even the Christmas feast was forbidden. The hearts of the villagers were very sad. Moreover,

[1] The origin of cricket. The game has been recently revived at Lords.

hateful informers were about. One, Robert May, received 18s. for "informing of one that played at trap-ball on the Lord's Day."

And worse was to follow. A new sport was devised, that of clergy-baiting. Committees were appointed to accomplish the ejection of the parsons from their livings. These committees encouraged "some factious neighbours to charge the clergy as being criminals, either in the way of drinking, idleness, negligence, etc., or else of insufficiency, and so they were accounted scandalous ministers." By false witnesses they injured the credit of the orthodox divines, and then proceeded to eject, plunder, and imprison them. The common gaols were full of them. The clergy were placed under hatches in small ships, with all holes stopped up that would give them air. It was proposed by these "pious" Puritans to sell them for slaves to the Turks. They were condemned by mock trials. During service time some troopers would seize the clergyman (as they did Dr. Turner at Fetcham), stamp on the Prayer-Book, put the surplice on one of the troopers tied round with an orange scarf, and march the vicar to prison. They then proceeded to ransack his house, destroy his library, and then turn out his wife and children, and introduce some wretched minister of their own, a common trooper and unordained, to hold the living. A wretch name Francis, of East Ilsley, dispossessed the Rev. Joseph Barnes, who had a wife and seven children. These were reduced to abject starvation, and one of the little girls went to Francis to ask for a crust of bread. The barbarous villain heard her tale, refused her request, and told her that "starving was as near a road to heaven as any other."[1]

Retributive justice befell most of these usurpers. The time came when the men of Merrie England had received a surfeit of Puritan customs, and their gentle ways and unbearable tyranny. They grew weary of these people who wore a sad-coloured dress, and who greeted everyone with sour looks and upturned eyes and a nasal whine. The villagers yearned for the good old days when there were dancing on the village green, and wrestling matches and Maypoles, and old Christmastide hospitalities, and all the old national pastimes. And when "the King enjoyed his own again," and had one grand triumphal procession from Dover to London, amidst the shouts and cheering of his people, in every village there was tumultuous rejoicing. The ringers rang a merry peal in the church tower, casks of ale were broached, flags waved, and joyful music sounded throughout the land. The intruding minister had to give place to the rightful rector, whom his people welcomed back with tumultuous joy, and there were few dry eyes in the congregation when he began to read again the old familiar service; and his voice almost failed him and the tears started when he read: "Great are the troubles of the righteous: but the Lord delivereth him out of all."

They did not all return. Some had died of starvation and misery; and the black-gowned in-

[1] See my book *The Old-Time Parson* for many other instances of abominable cruelty.

truding Puritan ministers lived on in the vicarages, to which they had succeeded by plunder or usurpation, and were thorns in the side of the Church for some time. They refused to comply with the doctrines and discipline of the Church. Many of them were not clergymen at all, mere mechanics, tradesfolk, troopers who had served in the rebel army and had taken up preaching. Others were outrageous fanatics and heretics, Independents, Anabaptists, Millennarians, and sectaries of many sorts. Is it conceivable that such men could have been permitted to act as parish priests, as clergymen of the Church of England ? They had to go. An Act of Uniformity was passed by Parliament in 1662, and the so-called " Black Bartholomew " day arrived, and sympathy is often asked for these men, and little shown to the ten thousand clergy of the Church of England, whose only fault was their loyalty to their King and Church, and who suffered during twenty years of wrong and spoliation.

A little story comes from Fetcham to show the diverse characters of the rector and his supplanter. Dr. Turner, a learned divine, whose name I have mentioned, was ejected by a mean wretch named Fisher. When the latter came to turn the rector out, Mrs. Turner was close upon her confinement, and he craved leave that his wife might stay till her trouble was over. This act of humanity Fisher refused, and the poor lady had to go in spite of her condition. Curiously enough, when Dr. Turner was restored to his own again, Fisher's wife was in a like state, and he made the like request. Dr.

Turner reminded him of his refusal, but added, "You shall see that I am a Christian. In the name of God let her tarry and welcome."

So the village woke again from its bad dreams. Retributive justice was seen in other directions. Take a case in point. During the Commonwealth Deans and Chapters of Cathedrals were suppressed, including Rochester. On the Dover Road there is a house called Jud's Folly. One Jud bought up cheaply some of the lands of the Chapter, made a good profit, and built for himself a fine house. At the Restoration the Chapter recovered its possessions, and with these the lands of Jud, whose fine house became the property of the Cathedral authorities, much to Jud's annoyance. His neighbours christened it Jud's Folly, though it bears now another name.

It cannot be said that the village prospered after the rejoicings of the Restoration. The coffers of the squires had been drained by the war and their loyal sacrifices. There was a want of capital. A large middle class had arisen, and these men set themselves to develop and improve their farms. Enclosures continued to be made. The Second Charles, who is credited with having "never said a foolish thing, and never did a wise one," certainly did one wise one. He accepted the proposals of Parliament with regard to purveyance, and the royal agents were no more seen with their carts in the village carrying off produce, hay and corn, cheese and butter, etc., nominally for the use of the Sovereign, but often for their own profit. There were great rejoicings in the village when the news came that purveyance was dead, and they drowned its remembrance in casks of ale. The old feudal rights had become obsolete, and had passed away; but the squires maintained their influence over their neighbouring tenants, yeomen, farmers, and labourers. They were active magistrates, useful in their generation, public-spirited and intellectual, courteous in their dealings with each other and compassionate to the poor. Their ranks had been recruited by the influx of many successful men, merchants, and traders from the towns, who had made money, bought estates, and founded families which were deemed county folk. Moreover, there had been a considerable infusion of foreign blood, the Flemish aristocracy contributing largely to swell the forces of their English neighbours. It was a gain to England when the Bentinck, Cavendish, Schomberg, Keppel families, and others, brought new ideas into the country.

The yeomen had increased in numbers and importance. They were freeholders, their lands passing to their heirs by right of inheritance. Every one respected them. The management of the affairs of the village was mainly in their hands. They were churchwardens, and under the chairmanship of the rector transacted most of the business of the parish in the vestry. They served on juries, as also did the copyholders.

Agriculture was improved by the efforts of such squires as John Evelyn and Jethro Tull, who made many inventions and revolutionised the farming industry. Nor did the squires fail to promote amusements in the village. I have here the diary of a Lancashire squire of the period. He records on one occasion the presence of sixty-four young people playing in a ring on his green, and about twenty spectators. They had "merry nights" at fairly frequent intervals in some barn, where a rustic ball took place to the cheerful tune of pipe and fiddle, and games were played: "chasing the whistle" and stool ball. The prize of the victors was a tansy, a dish made of eggs, sugar, sack, cream, and the juice of tansies fried in butter. There were grand festivals at flax-breaking and the flowering of the marl-pits. These were arranged by the squire himself and his family, and he took infinite pains to make the affairs pass off with éclat and enjoyment. I cannot tell you all his treats and festivities, his sword-dancing, his dinners, and will refer you to my former book, *The Old English Country Squire.*

The Church ended the century with triumph, and was never so popular as she was then. She was the champion of the liberties of England, when James II. tried to force on the country his Papistical ideas. You will remember the Trial of the Seven Bishops and its remarkable ending, and the people regarded the Church with gratitude and affection, as the saviour of the kingdom from regal tyranny and oppression, the protector of Protestantism and of freedom and liberty. Merry peals were rung in our village steeples when the news spread, and the parson was never more popular than he was then.

CHAPTER XVI

THE VILLAGE IN THE EIGHTEENTH CENTURY

Village orchestra—Killing vermin—The advent of William of Orange—Depressed state of the country—Heavy taxation—The condition of the poor—Squatters—*The Village Labourer*—Abuse of squires—Their charity—Dr. David Davies, Rector of Barkham—The Gilbert Act—Enclosing commons and lands—Effects of the new system—Gleaning—Middlemen's profits — Settlements — Riots — Poor Law—Workhouses—Speenhamland scheme and its fatal results.

IN looking back we are approaching more modern conditions, yet there is a vast amount of industrial, agricultural, and social problems that faces us in these later investigations. These can only be treated somewhat shortly, otherwise the size of this book will far exceed its original conception. The life of the village seemed to go on much as usual, and the Church enjoyed the affection of the people in the early part of the century. The evils of Pluralism were great, by which a fortunate parson could hold several livings, and leave a poorly paid curate to perform the duty. The churchwardens continued to be active, and kept their accounts regularly and accurately, and it is evident that at this period it became usual to form church bands or village orchestras to lead the singers during the services. The instruments they used were

Chiddingstone, Kent

the bassoon, violin, base viol, or violoncello, flute, clarionet, and hautbois. The bassoon gave much trouble, as it always wanted repairing: so the wardens' accounts show. The hautbois caused much difficulty in spelling, and sometimes appears as hautboy or haughtboy. I have told many stories of the achievements of the village orchestras in my book on *The Parish Clerk.* They were very popular, and though the music they produced was a little trying, they drew the men to church, and caused them to take a great interest in the services. The introduction of a harmonium or a barrel-organ made poor substitutes for the band. A merry peal of bells seems to have been rung on all suitable occasions, and England maintained its character as the "ringing isle."

The wardens seem to have been very busy slaughtering vermin and birds, and even—*mirabile dictu!*—dare I mention it? foxes. In some parishes as many as twenty were killed in one year, usually by a spring trap. Hedgehogs, ravens, sparrows, badgers, wild cats, blue tits, kites, and jays, were all included in the list of the victims preserved in these accounts. The killer of a fox or badger who brought the head to the church received 12d.; of a raven, 2d.; an otter, 6d. Rat-catchers and mole-catchers were regularly appointed, and war seeems to have been waged on all the feathered tribe.

Outside, national affairs disturbed but little the life of the village. Doubtless the rustics heard of the flight of King James and the advent of

William of Orange. There was more communication with the outside world than in former days. They attended the markets and heard the news; and the rector would discourse to them on Sundays about national events and point a moral on the King's attempts to enforce Romanism, and his fall and flight. They would hear of the Irish troops being brought over to England, and learn the story of the Reading skirmish and the tune of *Lillibalero* with the song:

Five hundred Papishes came there,
  To make a final end
Of all the town in time of Prayer,
  But God did them defend.

Perhaps if they lived in Devonshire, or Somerset, or Berkshire, they would actually see the Prince, whom their squire rode to meet, and whose army, with some of the farmers' sons, he would join. Possibly they saw the soldiers plundering the Chapel of the Eystons at East Hendred, and dressing up a "mawkin" in some of the vestments, and setting it up on the top of a bonfire. Queen Anne they would often see hunting with the Royal Buckhounds, and driving furiously in her chariot when she could no longer ride. Some of the lads of the village joined the army of the Duke of Marlborough in the Low Countries, "earning a fleeting glory e'en at the cannon's mouth," and would have much to tell of their experiences at the war, like our village youths of to-day who have fought in France and Italy, Salonika, Jerusalem, Mesopotamia, and elsewhere. But these were outside affairs, and did not prevent them from carrying on the chief things of life, the ploughing and sowing, reaping and mowing, the love-making and marrying, and earning a living.

This making a living was a mighty difficult thing. At the end of the seventeenth and beginning of the eighteenth century, it seemed that the nation was on the road to ruin, a road that is somewhat familiar to us modern folk. Trade was depressed; the national debt was high; and taxation heavy. Landlords could not get their rents, and farms were thrown on their hands. The woollen trade was decayed, and the workers were starving. Among the taxes people had to pay was the window tax, first devised in 1696, which all men hated. In old farmhouses to this day we constantly see windows blocked up with brickwork, relics of this obnoxious tax. Land tax was a heavy burden, as we still know to our cost. Landowners have always been saddled with the heaviest burdens of taxation, and at this time about one-third of their income they paid to the State, or 6s. 5d. in the £, whereas a London merchant only paid 2s. 4d.

Though the landowners were hard hit, the labourers were in a worse condition, in spite of the efforts made to relieve them. In no other country in Europe has more attention been given to the problems, and yet often the results have been lamentable. Norden in James I.'s time notes the building of cottages by wandering folk in waste places, who live hardly, do little work, dwelling far from a church, and who were as ignorant of God or of any civil course of life as the very savages amongst the infidels. The setting up of cottages by rogues and vagabonds in villages carefully selected on account of their good commons and convenient woods seems to have often been done at this time. By this means they secured a settlement, and were therefore entitled to poor relief according to the amended Acts of Elizabeth's reign. If they could prove a residence in a parish for forty days, their settlement was secure. So these crafty folk often hid themselves for that period, and, if undiscovered, they were safe and could claim their rights of maintenance. To obviate this fraud all intending squatters were obliged to have their names posted on the church doors before service on a Sunday morning, and the forty days were counted from that day. Hence the overseers had an opportunity for seeing whether the newcomers could obtain work, and be useful members of the community. Sometimes vagrants by plausible tales gained relief from the justices, in spite of the overseers; but this also was stopped by legal enactments. Then the authorities found that small parishes could not bear alone the burden of poor relief. So they formed groups of parishes after the fashion of the modern union. All sorts of arrangements were fashioned for the support of the genuine poor in contradistinction to that of rogues and vagabonds, and all proved feeble and ineffective. They did little to help the poor, and half ruined the farmers and landowners.

The whole story of the village and its labourers in the eighteenth and nineteenth centuries is one of the saddest chapters in our annals. It is all utterly deplorable, and I would gladly close this book, leaving the villagers happy and contented—dancing joyously on the village green, singing their cheery ballads, the carters and ploughmen whistling blithely as they drive their teams along, and the maidens singing as they spin, or as they go a-milking. A darkening pall seems to have fallen on the village; and misery, poverty, disease, and death, like grim spectres, have entered the cottage homes. It is all very grievous, but the tragedy must be told.

Several books have been written lately[1] which endeavour to throw the entire blame upon the aristocratic families who held the power in England during this period. The learned authors of *The Village Labourer* (*1760–1832*) set to work to prove that the squires exercised entire control in Parliament, in local government, that they regarded the sufferings and oppression of the poor with cynical neglect, and only thought of their own interests and of those of their class. Such a description of the character of the squires is misleading. Of course, in a body of such a large number of men there were "black sheep" as well as "white"; and the squires of that period, as in the former age, were not all aristocratic. Lawyers and merchants and tradesfolk had become landowners. As a class they had a considerable sense of the duty they owed to their country. They did a vast amount of entirely unpaid work. Those of them who wished

[1] *The Village Labourer*, by J. L. and B. Hammond. *English Local Government*, by S. and B. Webb. *The English Peasantry*, by G. Slater.

to become Members of Parliament had to spend vast fortunes in obtaining their seat. They were very charitable in giving money and food to the people in their villages. When they discovered the serious state of affairs the richer landowners tried, by private charity, to supplement the public poor-funds, and they organised "The Society for Bettering the Condition of the Poor"; and no one can glance at its Reports without discovering that very considerable effects were produced, and much beneficent effort made by the squires. Mr. Garnier in his *History of the English Landed Interest* states that the King, the gentry, and the clergy, vied with each other in bestowing comforts on those unable to purchase them, and tells of many instances where coals were supplied at prime cost, workrooms built for teaching spinning and weaving, general stores set up, flour, milk, etc., provided at a cheap rate. It is a mistake to suppose that nothing was done to improve the lamentable condition of the agricultural labourers.

In this same rectory wherein it is my lot to serve there lived one whose name should be honoured and remembered, the Rev. David Davies, D.D. (1743–1819), the author of a remarkable book, *The Care of the Labourers in Husbandry,* published in 1795. Professors of sociology and students of the social economy in England know well the value of my worthy predecessor's work. This book contains the results of the most careful and patient investigations, and made a profound impression on contemporary observers. Howlett called it "incomparable," and it is impossible for the modern reader to resist its atmosphere of reality and truth. Mr. Garnier remarks that no one before him had gone so deeply into the subject, and that he published some most interesting statistics relative to the economy of the cottages and the dietetics of its inhabitants, which probably did much to influence the policy of Pitt's administration. This country parson, whose sympathy was moved by the distress he saw around him, gives a simple, faithful, and sincere picture of the facts seen without illusion or prejudice, and free from all the conventional affectations of the time, a priceless legacy to those who are impatient of the generalisations with which the rich dismiss the poor.

What were his methods? When visiting his parishioners he was much distressed by their poverty, and he set himself to discover the causes that conduced to that result. He attributed them mainly to the high cost of provisions. He sets out in a table the weekly earnings and expenditure of six families in his parish, and then procured information from other parts of England which entirely supported his contention, and showed how difficult it was for the agricultural labourer to live. He earned 14d. a day, or 8s. a week, and his wife might earn 6d. In the first cottage there were five children unable to work. Every week the parents had to provide for bread or flour, 6s. 8d.; yeast and salt, 4d.; bacon or other meat, 8d.; tea, sugar, butter, 1s.; cheese and beer, seldom any; soap, starch, blue, 2½d.; candles, 3d.; thread, thrum, worsted, 3d.

The total sum per week amounted to 8s. 4½d., or £23 4s. 9d. per annum, his earnings coming to £22 2s. But besides the weekly expenses, rent, fuel, clothing, lying-in, etc., had to be paid for, and these amounted to £7 14s., making a yearly deficiency of £8 16s. 9d. Such was the poor labourer's lot in 1787. Few poor families could afford more than 1 lb. of meat, 1 or 1½ oz. of tea, ½ lb. of sugar, and ½ lb. of salt butter or lard per week. They could not buy milk or cheese. They could not brew any small beer, except against a lying-in or a christening. It was difficult to get soap for washing, so they burned the green fern, and kneaded the ashes into balls. A quarter of wheat then cost 48s. It was treble that amount later on, and the distress of the poor must have been greater still. If it had not been for the charity of the squire and the rector it is difficult to see how the labourers could have lived.

This worthy rector examined the records of antiquity, and showed by his tables how the labourers lived in the fourteenth, fifteenth, sixteenth, and seventeenth centuries. He examined and criticised the Poor Law that existed in his day, and found that it was extremely poor law. The Gilbert Act was then in force, and nearly ruined the ratepayers, without giving any satisfaction to the poor. He warned his contemporaries of the danger of the uncontrolled tendencies of the age. He objected to the depriving of the people of the grazing rights on the commons by the Enclosure Acts, as the rhymer states:

A sin it is in man or woman
To steal a goose from off a common;
But he doth sin without excuse
Who steals the common from the goose.

He objected to the engrossing of farms, the swallowing up of small farms by the larger farmers, and wrote:

Allow to the cottager a little land about his dwelling for keeping a cow, for planting potatoes, for raising flax or hemp. Secondly, convert the waste lands of the kingdom into small arable farms to be let to industrious families. Thirdly, restrain the engrossment and over-enlargement of farms. The propriety of these measures cannot, I think, be questioned.

Would that the authorities had immediately acted upon this good parson's advice. It would have saved the country from grievous troubles, and the labourers from much misery and semi-starvation if not actual. Let us look at the picture more closely, and try to discover the causes which converted a Merrie England into a very sad England, a prosperous, independent peasantry into a cowed and sullen race, and plenty into starvation.

One of the causes was undoubtedly enclosures. I have often referred to these, but before the eighteenth century the process of enclosure referred mainly to the bringing in of land taken from the wastes outside the village. England had still a large amount of open commons, where the villagers grazed their cows and geese and fowls, and common fields wherein labourers had their strips of land here and there, much the same as I have described in an earlier chapter. They had, in connection with these lands, rights and customs that had descended to them from the earliest times. A century later commons and common fields had for the most part disappeared and been swallowed up by large farms. The labourers had lost their inheritance. Forty years ago I was talking to an old labourer, and I said that I thought it was a pity that the commons had been enclosed. He replied in some such terms as these: "I regard England as a large country with crowds of people who have to be fed. The old commons were not much use to the country. A goose or two or a donkey fed there. It is better that the land should be made to produce as much as possible, and larger farms employ more men; so it was better for the labourer in the end."

The landlords and farmers in the eighteenth century were in entire agreement with my aged friend. They advocated enclosures everywhere. They thought they were conferring a great national benefit on the country by increasing the store of food. Large farms could be more economically worked than small farms. The political economists of the day, before the days of Adam Smith, all advised enclosures. Only by this means could agricultural progress be secured. The common-field system was the most wasteful form of farming possible. Land was wasted in balks and paths, and time was wasted in going from strip to strip. Bad and obsolete methods were in use. When the farmers wanted labourers to do some important work, the latter said they had to look after their own cows or dig their own land. They were very independent, and had their rights. Much better to throw all the fields into large farms.

So everyone thought, except the labourers, and they were the sufferers in this wholesale confiscation of the common lands. In vain did my worthy predecessor plead for land to be left to the poor. In vain did he protest against the engrossing of farms. It was all done for the good of the country, and so the labourers would be sure to find themselves better off in the end. As we study the Acts of Parliament, we find that effort after effort was made to better the condition of the poor, but they all seemed to end in failure, and the results were pitiful.

Under the old system every labourer by thrift and hard work could rise in the social scale. He could save his money and buy a little land, and gradually develop into a substantial farmer; under the new system he was doomed to drudgery, hopelessness and abject dependence. Under the old system the farmers complained that labourers were too independent, idle, and careless, and thought that when they had been deprived of their bits of land, their cows and pigs, they would be much more useful on the farm, and more subordinate. Some of these wiseacres and absurd thinkers objected to the kindness of a generous squire, who would often give a labourer a piece of ground and materials for him to build a house. By enclosure he lost his right of cutting fuel on the common, his bit of land, his cow and pig. Moreover, his privilege of gleaning after the harvest was stopped by the farmers. This was a valuable source of income, and a poor family would obtain by this means enough corn to last them through the winter. They read in their Bibles that Ruth gleaned after the reapers. They read also the passage in Leviticus, which enjoined: "And when ye reap the harvest of your land, thou shalt not make clean riddance of the corners of thy field when thou reapest, neither shalt thou gather any gleaning of thy harvest: thou shalt leave them unto the poor, and to the stranger." Their fathers and grandfathers had always enjoyed the privilege, and they did not understand why they should be prevented from gathering a little store to help them through the dreary and hard months of winter. But, owing to the rise in the price of corn, each ear was of value, and the poor were generally deprived of what they esteemed to have been their right of gleaning.

Again, my revered predecessor touches upon another hardship, which has not yet passed away—the excessive price which the poor had to pay for their provisions, owing to the profits of the middleman, or rather middlemen. The farmer sold his corn to the miller, the miller to the mealman, the mealman to the shopkeeper, and the last to the poor, who had thus to pay an enhanced price, especially as they could only afford to buy small quantities.

Then there was the vast subject of settlement, which became more complicated as the years sped on. In olden times, as we have seen, the villeins and labourers were confined to their own villages. They could not leave them in order to go and work for any other manor-lord than their own. Subsequently they obtained their freedom, and could work for any master and settle wherever they listed. When Poor Law enactments came in, the difficulty arose as to which parish should be obliged to relieve the destitute, and the theory of settlement had to be determined. This was decided to be the birthplace of the applicant for relief, or the place where he had worked for some years. But, as a matter of fact, there was little restraint on his movements until 1662, when an Act was passed limiting or destroying his liberty, and unless he could establish himself in a parish for forty days he was ejected and sent back to his former domicile. The whole business is very complicated, and would require much space for its full explanation. But the result of the Law of Settlement was that a labourer had to stay in his own village, to be content with the wages offered there, and have no power to go where higher wages could be obtained.

It will be gathered from the above that the lot of the labourer was not a happy one. There was universal discontent, and it is not surprising to find that there was some rioting in 1795, the very year that my revered predecessor's book was published. High prices were the chief cause. The rioting was not characterised by violence, and the women played the chief part. It was very orderly rioting. They knew that they were paying too high prices; so they resolved to seize the goods in the shops, and pay what they considered to be a fair and just charge. Our local newspaper, the *Reading*

Mercury, one of the oldest in the kingdom, records that at Aylesbury the women seized all the corn that came to market, and compelled the farmers to accept such prices as they thought proper. Similar scenes were enacted throughout the country.

This somewhat opened the eyes of the governing classes, and various expedients were adopted to relieve the distress. Some attempt was made to introduce less costly food, but this was rejected with scorn. Then we hear of the introduction of a minimum wage, of which we have heard much in recent times. The amount of wages was to be determined by the cost of food, which policy Dr. Davies advocated. The Whitbread Bill was brought into Parliament, but rejected. The discussion showed that in spite of the general poverty there had been a very large amount of private charity bestowed upon the poor; but in parishes where there was no resident squire the suffering was great.

Nor was the lot of the poor alleviated much by the Poor Law. As in modern times, there was outdoor and indoor relief. Workhouses were terrible places, much hated by the poor. It was called by various names and known as "the House," the Poor House, House of Maintenance, or House of Protection, or a Bettering House, but no change of name could make it acceptable to the poor, and no wonder, if Crabbe's description be a true one:

> Their's is yon house that holds the Parish-Poor,
> Whose walls of mud scarce bear the broken door;
> There, where the putrid vapours, flagging, play,
> And the dull wheel hums doleful through the day;

There Children dwell who know no Parent's care;
Parents, who know no Children's love, dwell there!
Heart-broken Matrons on their joyless bed,
Forsaken Wives and Mothers never wed;
Dejected Widows with unheeded tears,
And crippled Age with more than childhood fears;
The Lame, the Blind, and, far the happiest they!
The moping Idiot and the Madman gay.
Here, too, the Sick their final doom receive,
Here brought, amid the scenes of grief, to grieve,
Where the loud groans from some sad chamber flow,
Mixt with the clamours of the crowd below;
Here sorrowing, they each kindred sorrow scan,
And the cold charities of man to man:
Whose laws indeed for ruin'd Age provide,
And strong compulsion plucks the scrap from pride:
But still the scrap is brought with many a sigh,
And pride embitters what it can't deny.

Such were some of the awful places wherein these wretched people ended their days, but others were not so terrible. A workhouse at Wallingford formed a pleasant home for several young married couples, and there was an absolute scramble for rooms whenever a vacancy occurred. Attempts were made to amend the Poor Law, but most of these were failures. Then allotments were tried in some places, as in modern times; and where they were adopted the results were admirable. An example of this method is that of Sir Thomas Bernard's estate in Rutland, where " we have a picture of a little community leading a hard but energetic and independent life, the men going out to daily work, but busy in their spare hours with their cows, sheep, pigs, and gardens; the women and children looking after the livestock, spinning, or working in the gardens; a very different picture from that of the landless and ill-fed labourers elsewhere."[1] Similar successes were obtained in other places.

Then came the famous Speenhamland scheme, which raised that suburb of Newbury into unenviable notoriety. A meeting of Berkshire magistrates was held at the Pelican Inn, which a traveller once said was aptly named, as it had a very long bill, in 1795. They propounded a scheme for regulating wages according to the price of food; and this plan found favour in other counties, and though the wages were too low, and there was much discontent, all went well for a time while the high prices continued. But when the fall came in 1814, the house of cards tumbled down with alarming rapidity. It must be remembered that all classes of the agricultural community suffered at that time, when the war with France ended with the victory of Waterloo. Then, as now after the conclusion of the late war, everything was in confusion. Squires lost their estates, farmers were ruined, some became paupers, but the labourers were reduced to penury. Passions were aroused, and riots burst forth like a raging fire. In East Anglia mobs burned houses and ricks, and fights took place between the soldiers and the rioters, and with difficulty the rising was suppressed and the leaders were executed. Such is the sad story of decline, discontent, despair, desperation, and revolt.

[1] *The Village Labourer*, by J. L. and B. Hammond, p. 155.

CHAPTER XVII

THE VILLAGE IN THE NINETEENTH CENTURY AND IN MODERN TIMES

Improvement of agriculture—Jethro Tull—Lord Townshend—Arthur Young—George III.—Bakewell of Dishley—Coke of Norfolk—Condition of the Church—Parsons of the period—Gloom in the village—Poaching—Riots—Investigation of the conditions of labour—Poor Account Book of Barkham—Victorian era—Poor Law Reform of 1832—Agricultural societies—Friendly societies—Repeal of the Corn Laws—Riots—Villages no longer isolated—Coaching age—Games and sports—Cricket—Hunting—Oxford movement—Joseph Arch—Bad seasons—The squire—The War and after—The better England.

THE improvement of agriculture was an important event in village life during the eighteenth and nineteenth centuries. I have already mentioned the honoured name of Jethro Tull, our Berkshire farmer, who at the beginning of the eighteenth century invented the first drill that was ever used, and by his writings revolutionised agriculture. He had a farm called "Prosperous," though it brought little prosperity to its owner, near Inkpen, and there he practised his husbandry, and, as Cobbett states, "wrote that book which does so much honour to his memory, and to which the cultivators of England owe so much." This book was entitled, *Horse-hoeing Husbandry.* The main principle of the system first taught by Tull was that the root of the plant should be fed by deep tillage while it grows.[1] His ideas were far in advance of his times, and, like all inventors, he suffered from the opposition of his contemporaries, who opposed his theories and ridiculed his conclusions. His greatest trials resulted from the opposition of his own labourers, and he complained bitterly against them, because they thought that these new inventions would undermine labour; these men deliberately broke his machines, and refused to obey his orders. Though his book received little recognition in England, it was eagerly sought after in France, thrice translated within a few years of its publication, and Tull's husbandry was the basis of a work by M. de Hamel du Monceau, of the Royal Academy of Science in Paris. Tull's method of cultivating turnips was adopted by the Scottish farmers in 1760, and finally made its way back to Berkshire from that northern land.

Another great agricultural benefactor was Lord Townshend, who, after his retirement from State affairs in 1730, set to work as a farmer. He had been stationed in Hanover, whence he introduced to his estate at Rainham, in Norfolk, the cultivation of the turnip, and so revolutionised the industry. He earned the name of "Turnip Townshend," and was famous in every European country. No longer was the land allowed to lie fallow for a year, but by his four-course system every year it brought forth a crop. After a crop of wheat turnips were grown. This was followed by oats or barley, and then came

[1] An account of his work will be found in my account of "Agriculture" in the *Victorian History of Berkshire*, ii., p. 331.

clover or other grasses. By this means better sheep and cattle were produced, and the land fertilised. Arthur Young sounded his praises in no measured terms, and promised him fame, not as a statesman, but as a farmer.

Another famous name is Arthur Young himself, the son of a squire, who devoted himself to the study and perfecting of agriculture. He waged war against the ignorance and sloth of farmers, and strove to increase production. He was a scholar and a gentleman, and travelled extensively, using all his skill and brains and literary gifts for the diffusion of agricultural knowledge. It is impossible here to dwell on his career, his immense labours, the animosity of his critics, his struggles, trials, successes, and defeats, until at last his eyesight failed him, and he spent his last days in preaching religion to his Bradfield villagers. The country should never forget the services which Arthur Young rendered to the farmers of England.

An enthusiastic student of Young was "Farmer George," otherwise George III., who took the keenest interest in agriculture, revolutionised the farms at Windsor, and by his influence set a splendid example to the statesmen and country gentlemen of his time. I have referred to the Duke of Bedford, who started the draining of the Fens. His grandson, the fifth Duke, experimented greatly in farming, and was the founder of Agricultural Shows. Another great improver of farming was Bakewell, of Dishley, who set himself to improve the breed of stock, especially sheep. He was the prototype of John Bull, as depicted by Leech, and to his farm flocked crowds of agriculturists from all parts of England and abroad to examine his methods and learn the lessons that he taught.

One of the most famous names in agricultural history is that of Thomas Coke, of Norfolk, one of the best of landlords, the owner of a great estate, Member of Parliament, who devoted himself to the study of farming, and in diffusing his knowledge among his tenants and neighbours. He began by taking up a poor and impoverished farm on his estate, experimented there, extended his farm, studied its problems, and then used to gather his tenants about him and show them how they might increase their incomes and improve their farms. Experts from all parts of Europe used to come to his famous sheep-shearing festivals. Five hundred guests would sit down to dinner in his hall. New farm-buildings and cottages graced his estate, and his influence extended far beyond the boundaries of his own county.

These are only some few examples which might be mentioned of the beneficent efforts of the squires and aristocracy in benefiting agriculture, and in improving the conditions of village life by removing ignorance and old-fashioned methods, and in increasing the prosperity of the countryside.

When last I wrote of the Church, it was in the height of popular esteem, but for several reasons, which I have no space to describe, the clergy had in the main lost their popularity. There was a splendid array of learned clergy who wrote books on the defence of Christianity, and during the whole course of the long history of the Church no greater number of first-class works of the highest kind on controversial theology were written than during this period. But the country clergy were generally slack in doing their duty to their parishioners. There were many exceptions, and a parson's good deeds are seldom recorded, while his evil deeds or carelessness are often retold. But there was little life in the Church, and it failed to stem the irreligion and immorality that prevailed to a fearful extent. But a better time soon dawned. There was a great religious revival when the early Methodists began their work; and though, owing to the mistaken course of the Bishops, the movement separated itself from the Church, Methodism sprang from the heart of the Church herself, and John Wesley, Berridge, Whitefield, and others, were her ministers. The great Evangelical movement followed, and wrought wonders in improving the morals of the age and the conduct of both clergy and people.

The parsons of the period were many of them gentlemen; some were the sons of the squires and held family livings, and others were born in a parsonage, or came from tradesfolk or merchant stock. As domestic chaplains and tutors to the children of the manor-house or mansion they were brought into intimate connexion with the nobility and county families. They mixed with all classes of society, not excluding the poor, to whom they were kind friends and neighbours, if not particularly elevating spiritual guides. They took part in the sports of the gentry, fished, hunted, and shot with them, farmed and attended markets and fairs with them, and their dress was not dissimilar. Some of them were very poor, like Dr. Primrose, "the Vicar of Wakefield," who would go to the fair to sell his colt, and have a friendly glass with the purchaser at the inn; and others were rich, like Dr. Taylor, of Ashbourne, described by Boswell, who had a coach with four horses, a fine establishment, and when the winter was severe gave £200 to the poor. It is a mistake to suppose that the clergy neglected the poor or did not sympathise with their sufferings in the days of dearth. They started Sunday-schools in this period, and I find that my revered predecessor, Dr. Davies, used to pay for the education of several children in a day-school. Then, as now, the poor found in their parson their best friend, though it was impossible for him to remove the hardships and bad system of local government under which they lived.

Meanwhile, gloom reigned in the village. The people were poor and oppressed. There were the stocks and whipping-post on the green waiting for malefactors—a drunken husband, or a scolding wife. The old sports were dead. Sheridan and Cobbett had tried to revive them, but the lingering taint of Puritanism and the depressed spirits of the people prevented their success. One sport they indulged in, and that was poaching, in spite of the heavy penalties inflicted upon those who were caught. When a young man who was breaking stones on the roadside was asked how he managed to live on half-a-crown a week, he said, "I don't live on it. I poach: it is better to be hanged than starved to death." These poachers went about in gangs, and fought with and often killed the keepers. Lawlessness pervaded the country. There were bands who blacked their faces at Waltham, Wokingham, and elsewhere. They were called the Waltham Blacks, and the Wokingham Blacks, and levied blackmail on the farmers and cottagers. Sir John Cope fined one of the gang at Bramshill, and the same night hundreds of acres of his plantations were fired, and destroyed. They murdered many, and were with the utmost difficulty caught and convicted, hanged, or transported. The deer that roamed wild in Windsor Forest were caught with a hooked apple in an orchard; the poachers armed with guns shot and wounded or killed the keepers. In the Forest it was not all want and starvation that made poachers. There was wild blood in the veins of these men, and an innate love of sport, which led them on; but in most parts of England low wages, the miserable Poor Law system, and other defects bred lawlessness, which vindictive sentences and harsh punishments failed to uproot.

It is not surprising that riots often broke out. There were disturbances in 1795 and in 1816 which were suppressed; but, like the fires on our heath commons, apparently subdued for a time, they often broke out again. Occasionally ricks were fired and destruction done, but in 1830 a formidable rural insurrection arose which alarmed the country. The labourers, exasperated into madness by insufficient food and clothing, by utter want of necessaries for themselves and their families, began a revolt. Hateful workhouses, ricks, barns, the new-fangled machines for saving labour, such as threshing-machines, which the people thought took bread out of the mouths of starving folk, were consigned to the flames. Kent was the scene of the first exploits of the rioters, but they soon extended to Sussex, and later to Surrey, Berkshire, Hampshire, and Wiltshire, Dorset, Gloucestershire, East Anglia, and to many other counties. An immense amount of damage was done; farmers, landowners, and the clergy were frightened out of their lives. Beyond burning barns the rioters were not unreasonable in their demands. They compelled the farmers to give higher wages, the parsons to lessen the tithe, the tradesmen to reduce the price of food. The most obnoxious persons in the parishes were the overseers, who had been the chief oppressors of the poor, tyrants, and bullies; these men the labourers in several cases placed in dung-carts, and expelled them from the villages. Sometimes the parson would act as mediator between the labourers and farmers, and arrange terms of agreement.

Alas, the affairs became worse! Violence increased; the Government became alarmed; repressive measures were taken. The yeomanry and special constables were called out; leaders arrested; judges sent through the shires to try offenders. Some were executed, many transported or imprisoned in England; the jails were full; but at length order was more or less restored, and the revolt of the labourers brought to them little benefit, while it entailed terrible suffering, hardship, and death to many who took part therein. Some writers have dilated upon the terrors and cruelties of transportation, but a prison chaplain records that hardened offenders were delighted to be sent where they said they could get good food and lightish work, and were bitterly disappointed if their crime was only bad enough to involve hard labour at home.

As a result of the riots a very careful investigation was made of the conditions of labour. The general impression gathered from this report is that labourers at this time were badly paid, hired as a rule from week to week, the farmers hoping to keep down the rates by avoiding the labourers' settlement; that all but quite small families were kept by the parish; that considerable discontent existed, and much bad feeling between masters and men; that, as I have stated, actual riots and machine-breaking had taken place. Some amusing instances of the general slackness of the time and the dependence on the rates appear in the reports of the commissioners. At Ashbury on the Berkshire Downs a pauper who was lame bought a horse, in order that he might ride daily to the stone-pit, whilst a pauper wedding at Compton was quite a grand affair, costing the parish £6 15s. 4½d. We constantly find such entries as: To Elizabeth for kindness to her father, 5s.; to Lucy for looking after her ill mother, 3s. 6d. At Caversham 5s. was paid to William Dormer, ill (through drink)! One overseer tried to reduce the parish expenditure by suggesting that a bell need not be tolled at the death of every pauper, but when the parish clerk threatened to fight him he abandoned his vain attempt at saving the rates.

No wonder the rates were high. Happily the Parish Poor Account Book (1794–1829), in my village of Barkham, is in my possession. The population was then 180. The rate in 1794 was

3s. 6d. in the £. In 1800 it was 13s. 6d., when Dr. Davies wrote in his good handwriting that the large sum of £533 11s. 9d. was expended on the poor—a huge sum. It would be interesting to publish these items of expenditure, but want of space forbids. When people were ill they always received 5s. or 12s.; the overseer paid 9s. 5d. to Mr. Heelas (in Wokingham, whose draper's shop still remains) for Martha Brant's clothes. He paid for cutting turf for the parish, for the services of a midwife and of a doctor, cloth for the poor, coach higher (hire), and the expenses of Joseph Web and family (£1 15s.), Dame Parker for "nursen" Dame Wise, an apron for Lacey girl, for 22 pints of Beer for Thomas Hunt when ill, for shoes and boots, breeches and waistcotes, calico and linen. When a girl went into service her outfit was provided (*e.g.*, "Hutt's girl going to service, £1"). The overseer gave bread and cheese and beer at funerals, for laying out the corpse. "To make bread money" is difficult to understand. The overseers paid for mending shoes—*e.g.*, "Paid for mending Dame Pally's shoes, 2s. 6d."; for sheets, for thatching cottages, for cutting turf for firing, for soap and candles, rents, washing and mending, pecks of malt, and much else that I cannot now enumerate. The impression to be derived from a study in this book is that the people were extraordinarily well looked after and cared for, and that the overseers' office was no sinecure. He received the modest sum of £5 for his labours, and the petty constable two guineas.

Looking backwards over the last century we notice

many changes in rural life. In the early years of the Victorian era the farmers were prosperous, and the labourers benefited. Though wages were low, they had many perquisites. By piece-work they could earn, working early and late, about 5s. a day, though the average wage was generally much lower. An aged farmer friend, aged eighty, tells me that in his native county, Devonshire, he knew in his boyhood many labouring men who had raised themselves by their thrift and hard work to the position of tenant farmers, holding two hundred or three hundred acres. In 1834 the odious Speenhamland scheme was abolished by the passing of the Poor Law Amendment Act, and this had a good effect. It reduced the poor-rate enormously. Unions of groups of parishes were formed into one workhouse for the whole union; outdoor relief was abolished, except for the aged, the infirm, widows, and orphans; and lazy, able-bodied men who would not work were brought into the house and there set to work. The labourers liked the new scheme, and it is reported that they were more civil and contented.

Agricultural Societies were formed in some counties. In Berkshire one was established as early as 1794, then prizes were given to the best ploughman, the best sheep-shearer, to servants who had remained the longest time in the same situations, and to the largest families brought up without the aid of parish relief. In the nineteenth century in several counties Friendly Societies were established, and encouraged thrift and saving. Bequests for charitable uses were constantly being founded, especially in the eighteenth century, and old charities constantly received additions.

The price of corn remained high, and there was a great agitation in the forties for the Repeal of the Corn Laws. The "hungry forties" caused much distress, and I have talked with men who, as boys, remember the hard times, the dearness and scarcity of food, which, in some measure, was relieved by the charity of the squires and well-to-do farmers. In my own parish there was a Lady Bountiful, Mrs. Clive, who seems to have fed and run the whole village. There was a considerable opposition on the part of the landlords and farmers to the Repeal, and Anti-Corn Law Repeal Leagues were founded. Coke, of Norfolk, was strongly opposed to the Repeal, and when he was discovered one day in Norwich market the crowd attacked him, and he would have fared ill had not a man named Kent released a raging bull which scattered the crowd; the Riot Act was read, and the riot dispersed. At that time riots and machine-burning were features of agricultural life. But the Repeal was passed in 1849; the price of corn diminished, and the farmers saw that their only salvation consisted in reducing the cost of production, in using labour-saving machines, and in improving the methods of farming.

In the meantime many changes had come to the village. It was no longer an isolated community, but had been brought into contact with the great world. Before the revolution wrought by railways all the villages on the great roads were inundated by coaches and carriages and ceaseless traffic. It would take too long to recall the story of the roads themselves, how they were rescued from being mere "sloughs of despond" by the genius of Telford and Macadam, harnessed by toll-gates, and lined by inns which had stables for hundreds of horses, and travellers lodged in the village inns, and the familiar figures of the cheery coachmen and the sound of the guard's horn startled the peace of the hamlets, and brought life and animation to the village. Although hard times and Puritanism had damped the old-fashioned merriment of rural life, though church ales and suchlike relaxations were things of the past, the social amusements and love of games natural to English folk to some extent survived. Morris-dancing, Whitsuntide revels, Hocktide customs, harvest festivals, Plough Monday sports, Christmas mumming, and much else, lived on. Rustic cricket began to flourish, and such matches as are described by Miss Mitford took place in many villages. Cruel sports were not yet dead, and bull-baiting and cock-fighting were indulged in by squires and farmers, affording amusement to townsfolk and villagers. Hunting became a highly systemised sport. Instead of trencher-fed packs, each farmer keeping and contributing two or more hounds, regular kennels were established by keen squires, such as Sir John Cope, of Bramshill, and the labourers were almost as much interested in the sport as the members of the hunt. Many of the clergy, such as Charles Kingsley, Jack Russell, and others, rode to hounds, and in doing so in no way sacrificed the good opinion of their parishioners, whatever may be the opinion of the present generation with regard to hunting parsons. No one loved and laboured for the poor more than Kingsley, and no one enjoyed more than he a run with the hounds. A higher conception of the duties of the clerical office, and perhaps also a certain "tightness of the chest," as Russell styled clerical poverty, have weened parsons from the hunting field, and by the Oxford Movement new life has been infused into the old church, and brought many blessings to the villagers. Pluralism, that great enemy of efficiency, has long ago been slain, and it has been an immense advantage to each village to have an educated man and spiritual guide living amongst the people, one who not only ministers to them in spiritual things, but who is also the friend, helper, and adviser of everyone in the place. By the dethronement of the powers of the old vestry and their transference to Parish Councils, it might be thought that the parson's influence is greatly diminished; but that is scarcely so, as the rector is usually the chairman of the Parish Council, which carries on the work of the more ancient body without much change. Nonconformity has found its way into many villages. There have been cases of rivalry sometimes, sometimes even bitterness; but all that is happily for the most part at an end, and if some form of reunion between Church and Chapel could be arranged, it would be a satisfaction to many Churchmen.

In southern England wages continued low, though in the North they were raised. During the Franco-Prussian War the farmers prospered, and they were rather ashamed of themselves that they did not increase the limited and meagre wage of their employees. But usually a good feeling existed between them. The men had many perquisites, and often received gifts and gratuities in cases of sickness and distress. But in 1871 the labourers' champion arose in the person of Joseph Arch, who aroused the spirit of the men and encouraged discontent. He had many sympathisers among the clergy. Bishop Fraser, of Manchester, earned the title of the "Archbishop," and my friend the Hon. James Leigh, afterwards Dean of Hereford, took a prominent part in his pilgrimages throughout England for the purpose of founding the National Agricultural Labourers' Union. There were strikes in many parts of England during harvest-time, the labourers refusing to gather in the corn until they received larger wages. These were obtained, but, unfortunately, with the result of severing the kindly relationship between the farmers and the men, the promotion of discontent, and the emigration of many families to the Colonies.

However, the conditions of the village were fairly satisfactory at that period. Landlords set themselves to improve the housing of the cottagers. Many erected greatly improved dwellings. In my own neighbourhood the teaching of Charles Kingsley bore fruit. His pupil, Mr. Martineau, used to build model cottages every year. Mr. Walter and Lord Wantage built largely and well, and in many other parts of England the same process was going on. But several disastrous seasons followed, which brought much distress to English agriculture.

The seasons were bad. Corn dropped to 30s. a

quarter, and even less. In former times, when a bad harvest occurred, the farmers, as Lord Beaconsfield said, " enjoyed the dismal consolation of high prices "; but when England was flooded with corn from abroad, no such high prices reconciled the farmers to the scantiness of their crops. Many were ruined. The landlords reduced the rents to very nominal values, and were themselves impoverished, while they gazed upon their once smiling fields, now derelict or turned into pasture. In the vicinity of towns dairy farmers were more fortunate than others, and the railways to London and the great provincial towns became " milky ways " inundated with milk cans.

When the twentieth century dawned agriculture improved somewhat, but the passing of legislative Acts imposing heavy taxes upon landowners has obliged many old families, which have held their estates for centuries to sell their lands, and these have passed into the hands of men who have made their fortunes by trade, and who are ill-suited to occupy the position of squires. The old squire was an upright magistrate, a kind landlord, a liberal contributor, according to his means, and in later days above his means, to every judicious plan of charity. He was the friend of the poor, the unflinching protector of the oppressed, the firm opponent of the wicked, ever willing to advise, ever ready to help; bold to warn the profligate, kind to encourage the industrious. He was a very busy man. Chairman of the Board of Guardians, of the Quarter Sessions, he never missed a meeting, or came late. He devoted a certain part of his day to receiving people who came to him for advice on the many matters that concern rural economy. He was personally active in the promotion of education amongst the poor, and long before the State began to educate the children of the poor he built a little school and paid the salary of the mistress. He took an active interest in the support of all religious societies in the neighbouring town, and applied his mind to understand all subjects connected with the well-being of the poor, directing the management of clubs, allotments, benefit societies, etc. He was never absent from his family pew in church either morning or afternoon on Sundays. At home, on the Bench, in the vestry of his parish, on the Board of his Union, in the cottage of the poor, and at the table of his neighbours, serving on all manner of philanthropic boards, the leader of all social functions and neighbouring sports, he was ever treated with respectful homage. This is not a mere fancy portrait. In the sixties, when a German professor visited England and stayed with Mr. Barwick Lloyd Baker, of Hardwicke Court, Gloucestershire, and closely observed his mode of life and his activities for the public good, he was astonished, and said to a friend, "If in every English county there were three men like Mr. Baker to be found, I should envy your country far more on that account than for those gigantic golden millions that are hoarded up in the vaults of the Bank of England."

But the race is dying out. New times, new manners, and those who have taken their place are poor substitutes for the old squire. Though not ill-disposed they are ignorant of country customs and the deep-seated feelings of country folk. Money cannot buy the position of the ancient squirearchy. Millionaires have bought up large portions of the country, and I suppose the process must continue, but I have yet to meet one who ever purchased, with the title, the affections of its inhabitants, and Midas, profiteerer, or the inventor of a new kind of soap or sausages, is a sore infliction. But the revolution has begun, quiet and peaceful, with no outward signs of violence and disturbance; but it is no less a revolution. We who live in the country know well the resulting evils. Before the war came the uncertainty of securing labour, the feeling of insecurity and distrust, the passing away of the guiding hand that had steered the village community through times of stress and difficulty, the dread of future troubles—all this was sorely felt in the agricultural parts of the country.

The war came as a bombshell upon the life of the village. Many of our young men volunteered for active service with commendable patriotism. Others were called up, and have proved themselves to be the best of soldiers. They have fought on every front, and men from my own parish have upheld the honour of England in France, Italy, Macedonia, Egypt, Palestine, Syria, Mesopotamia, as well as in the Navy, amidst the fiery ordeal of Zeebrugge. And, thank God! most of them have returned with their varied experiences, which must make ordinary village life, with its ploughing and sowing, reaping and mowing, seem to them rather dull. But they are happy to be back amongst us once more, and take kindly to their former occupations.

A new page is opened in our village history, a new scene is presented. During the war the price of corn has risen enormously. Old pastures have been ploughed up; England has done its best to provide her children with corn grown in her own fields, and the farmers have risen nobly to supply her needs. Labourers have been rewarded with adequate wages, which appear to be magnificent when compared with the pittance earned by their grandsires, though, alas, high prices have considerably modified the benefit!

A new era has dawned upon our village life. We can never be quite the same again. There are many problems to be solved in the future, many dangers that threaten our happiness, prosperity, and peace. We ask ourselves how long the high prices of agricultural produce can be maintained, bring prosperity to the farmers, and enable them to pay the high wages that they are now bound to pay. Will they feel compelled to reduce the number of their labourers and permit the cornfields again to relapse into pasture? Too long have the various Governments neglected us. They thought little about us when our farmers were being ruined by foreign competition, and our labourers were but poorly paid. Now we are very much in evidence. They have begun to see that we were poorly housed, that our cottages were mean and often unfit to live in. Now we have housing schemes provided for us, and small holdings have been started, so that everyone may raise himself if he will, farm his twenty or forty acres, and have his own cows and pigs and sheep and poultry. This will do much to restore to the labourer the advantages of which the Enclosure Acts deprived him, and give to him that which my revered predecessor, Dr. Davies, advocated more than a century ago.

Most self-respecting villages now possess a club and reading-room, and whist drives and other forms of rational amusement are as common as blackberries. The war has killed our cricket and football clubs, but they are gradually being revived. The new Education Act has given opportunities for clever children of labourers to rise in the social scale and obtain work suitable for their talents. Lectures in the winter evenings and concerts make the long nights less drear; the revival of old folk dances and song, of village acting and pageantry, are not without their influence; and in all these schemes the Church takes a prominent part, helping, arranging, organising, while the village House of God is becoming more and more what it was in former days, the home of the people.

Such a picture of the state of the village we trust is being gradually painted in many a hamlet of rural England. It is a part of that "better England" of which we have all been straining our eyes to catch a glimpse, and for which many a brave and gallant son has laid down his life and made the last supreme sacrifice. This pledges us to use every effort to carry on the work of the reconstruction of village life.

> And us they trusted; we the task inherit,
> The unfinished task for which their lives were spent;
> But leaving us a portion of their spirit,
> They gave their witness and they died content.
> Full well they knew they could not build without us
> That better country, faint, and far descried,
> God's own true England, but they did not doubt us—
> And in that Faith they died.

APPENDIX

STONEHENGE (PAGE 30)

SINCE the first edition of this book was issued much has happened. Men have been employed by the Office of Works, and are raising the fallen Monoliths, placing the lintels on the Trilithons, and restoring the monument to its former condition. Several important discoveries have been made, amongst them the "Aubrey Holes," a series of holes probably made in Neolithic times for the erection of a stone circle earlier than the present structure. Cremated human remains have been found in these holes. All the puzzles connected with Stonehenge have not yet been solved. Sir William Boyd Dawkins is of opinion that the blue "mystery" stones could not have been conveyed by glacial action, as he believes no part of Britain south of a line drawn between Bristol and London was ever under ice. The stones must have been brought from Wales or Cornwall, or the Channel Isles. Bygone archæologists used to associate Stonehenge with Druidism, and named one important stone the "Slaughtering Stone," imagining that on it the Druids killed their victims. But Stonehenge belongs to an epoch far earlier than Druidism. It is undoubtedly connected with the religion of the primitive folk who contrived to rear its massive stones, and with the burial of their dead whose remains lie around in countless barrows.

INDEX

PRINTED IN GREAT BRITAIN BY BILLING AND SONS, LTD., GUILDFORD AND ESHER